Dear Alyssa,

Thank you again for letting us use your room. We appreciate your unselfishness. You are a beautiful girl, and we love you very much.

I thought you might enjoy these short thought and be able to use them in talks and just give guidance and encouragement each day.

Pres. Kimball's love for all people and down-to-earth lifestyle has always made me love him.

I hope you will get acquainted with him through this little book.

Love
Grandma + Grandpa Douglas

A PROPHET'S
VOICE

INSPIRING QUOTES FROM
SPENCER W.
KIMBALL

A PROPHET'S
VOICE

INSPIRING QUOTES FROM
SPENCER W.
KIMBALL

Covenant Communications, Inc.

Cover painting by Roscoe A. Grover.

Cover design copyrighted 2007 by Covenant Communications, Inc.

Published by Covenant Communications, Inc.
American Fork, Utah

Printed in Canada
First Printing: January 2007

12 11 10 09 08 07   10 9 8 7 6 5 4 3 2 1

ISBN 978-1-59811-307-5

TABLE OF CONTENTS

SOURCES AND ABBREVIATIONS

Faith   *Faith Precedes the Miracle.* 1972.

Miracle   *The Miracle of Forgiveness.* 1969.

Speaks   *President Kimball Speaks Out.*
                 1981.

Youth   *Youth of the Noble Birthright.*
                 1960.

THE PROPHET

Spencer W. Kimball, the sixth of Andrew and Olive Woolley Kimball's eleven children, was born March 28, 1895, in a modest brick home in Salt Lake City, Utah. At the time of Spencer's birth, Andrew was serving as the part-time president of the Indian Territory Mission (in present-day Oklahoma); between trips by train to visit his missionaries, he sold salt, soap, and candy throughout Utah and southern Idaho to support his family. Shortly before Spencer turned three, Andrew was released as mission president and called by President Wilford Woodruff to be president of the St. Joseph Stake in southeastern Arizona's Gila Valley—a calling he held until his death twenty-six years later.

Hard work and irrigation had made Gila Valley a green pocket of productive farm land. Andrew rented a three-room house constructed of adobe bricks and pitched a white tent, called "The White House," in the yard to accommodate his growing family of eight. Residents of Thatcher gave the Kimballs ten acres of land and helped dig out chaparral, greasewood, and hundreds of mesquite trees to make it suitable for farming. Sporting a miniature pitchfork, Spencer loved to work at Andrew's side.

His early years in Thatcher taught young Spencer values he would rely on for a lifetime. Though Andrew worked hard at a variety of occupations, the time he dedicated to the welfare of the several thousand members of his stake often left just enough income for his family to get by on. As a result, Spencer learned the value of thrift—wearing hand-me-down clothing and straightening out bent nails so they could be re-used. Growing up in an area dependent on rain to feed the river for vital irrigation, he learned the value of fasting and prayer. And he first learned about tithing while walking with his mother to deliver the tithing eggs to the bishop—a lesson that was later reinforced as he and his brothers gathered each tenth load of hay from the very best part of the field.

Young Spencer also learned the value of work by gathering potatoes in a little red wagon and selling them to the hotel kitchen. At lunchtime he usually ran the three blocks home from school to feed the pigs and pump the water for the cows before eating his lunch and dashing back to school. And work on the farm seemed never to end. He was in charge of feeding and watering the animals—sometimes as many as fifty pigs at a time—and milking the cows, as well as helping his older brothers harvest the hay.

On Spencer's eighth birthday, his father baptized him in a large metal vat the family occasionally used as a bathtub. When someone voiced concern four years later that Andrew had not gone down into the water with his son during the baptism, Spencer was baptized again in the Union Canal—just to be sure.

The family struggled with illness. Three of his sisters died while he was just a boy; he himself spent seven weeks in bed with a "mild" case of the typhoid fever that killed many in Thatcher. And when he was eleven, Spencer's mother died while pregnant with her twelfth child.

Andrew later married Josephine Cluff, one of Olive's friends whose own children were grown.

Spencer took his priesthood assignments seriously; as a deacon, he used a horse and buggy to collect fast offerings, which often consisted of honey, squash, or bottles of fruit. At the age of fourteen, he taught a Sunday School class. About the same time, Susa Young Gates asked a capacity crowd at stake conference how many had read the Bible all the way through. When only a few hands went up, Spencer took on the challenge for himself. He went home, lighted the coal-oil lamp in his attic bedroom, and began reading. Faithfully reading a few pages a day, he met his goal a year later.

After graduating from grade school, Spencer attended the Church-sponsored Academy, where he served as class president every year and was practically a straight-A student (he received his only B in chemistry). He and his friends formed an orchestra in which he played the piano. During his senior year he was the smallest but quickest member of the Academy basketball team—which, in a game at the Thatcher meetinghouse, defeated the University of Arizona basketball team. Spencer credited the victory to the fact that his team regularly played there and knew how to shoot low enough to avoid the overhanging beams.

At his graduation ceremony, Spencer was stunned to hear his father announce over the podium that instead of going to college, Spencer would be serving a mission. He hadn't really given it much immediate thought, since most missionaries at that time were older men, but he embraced the formal call when it arrived from Salt Lake City. To finance his mission he sold his horse, and spent the summer working at a dairy near Globe, Arizona. The eighteen-hour days were grueling, but at the end of the summer the cigar-smoking non-Mormon dairy owner threw a party for Spencer and gave him a gold watch to take on his mission.

Spencer left for Missouri at nineteen, younger than most, at a time when missionaries still traveled "without purse or scrip." After teaching in a schoolhouse one night, Spencer and his companion asked for a bed. In response, a family of eight led the two missionaries down a seemingly endless path through the dark woods to a one-room shack. The mother and five children climbed into the loft, and the father and his son shared a cot—giving Spencer and his companion the only bed in the house. They had given a widow's mite, sacrificing all they had for the elders.

Following his mission, Spencer attended the University of Arizona, then transferred to Brigham Young University. With so many young men enlisted in World War I, his classes were small—six in theology, four in history, two in math, and Spencer was the only student in his public speaking class. Within a few days of arriving at BYU, he received a notice that he needed to take a physical exam and report for military duty with the next group of soldiers organized from his community.

He returned to Thatcher—too late to ship out with the group that had been deployed, but just in time to resume courting Camilla Eyring, who had come to Thatcher to teach high school at the Academy. After just a few weeks, the two decided to marry. Unable to travel to Salt Lake for a temple wedding, they married at Camilla's home on Friday, November 16, 1917—Spencer in his khaki uniform, Camilla in a pink party dress. When the army did not call up Spencer immediately, he got a job in a bank and spent seven dollars out of his first paycheck to buy Camilla a simple wedding ring. By June, when the Academy let out for the summer, they had saved enough money to travel by train to be sealed in the Salt Lake Temple.

That summer Camilla completed her school contract bouncing over rough roads in a Model T Ford, enduring the hot Arizona sun to visit students who were completing their schoolwork at home. Late that August they welcomed their first child, Spencer LeVan. When World War I ended on November 11, 1918, Spencer took on two additional jobs—as a bookkeeper for a store and as stake clerk (then a paid part-time position)—to support his young family. Within four years, they had saved enough to buy a new car and make the down payment on their first home. They also welcomed their second child, a blond blue-eyed girl named Olive Beth, after Spencer's mother.

In 1924, Andrew's health was failing, and he moved to Salt Lake City, where better medical care was available. When it appeared the end was near, Spencer took a leave of absence from his job to be with his father. He spent long nights holding Andrew's hand while Andrew agonized and pleaded with the Lord to let him die.

When at last the longed-for peace occurred, President Heber J. Grant traveled with Spencer to return Andrew's body to Thatcher for burial. As his father's casket was lowered into the ground next to Olive, Spencer broke down and sobbed almost uncontrollably. Both of his parents and five sisters were gone. Spencer was twenty-nine.

While in Arizona, President Grant called a special conference to reorganize the stake presidency, and Spencer W. Kimball was sustained as first counselor. His older brothers pleaded with President Grant that such a responsibility was too great for one so young, but President Grant ended the discussion by saying, "Spencer has been called to this work, and he can do as he pleases about it." Spencer never considered refusing the call; he would never do less than his best in serving the Lord. For several years he served as both counselor and stake clerk.

In 1927, the Kimballs welcomed their third child and named him Andrew Eyring after Spencer's father. Spencer went into business with Bishop Joseph Greenhalgh. The Kimball-Greenhalgh insurance and real estate agency opened for business in a tiny office in back of the bank. Their insurance sign read, "See us before you buy, burn, or die." During the next few years, the company grew enough to invest in a subdivision planned for eighty-two houses. After the fledgling business poured sidewalks and curbs, planted trees, and sold a few lots, the stock market crashed and the nation plunged into the Great Depression. Business ground to a halt.

With cash scarce, people turned to trading—and since storekeepers needed insurance, they gave Kimball-Greenhalgh credit. So when Camilla needed merchandise, she'd find out which stores owed Spencer money.

In 1930, the Kimballs had their fourth child, a red-headed boy they named Edward after Camilla's father. Shortly after that, the bank closed its doors, taking with it thousands of dollars belonging to Kimball-Greenhalgh, the St. Joseph Stake, and various other organizations for which Spencer served as secretary. Despite continued economic problems, Kimball-Greenhalgh managed to stay afloat.

Shortly before Edward's third birthday, he fell ill and was rushed to California, where he was diagnosed with polio. For years afterward, the family traveled to California every summer so Eddie could have surgeries on his legs.

When Elder Melvin J. Ballard divided the St. Joseph Stake several years later, Spencer was called to be the president of the newly organized Mount Graham Stake. The stake boundaries extended from southeastern Arizona across southern New Mexico and as far as El Paso, Texas.

In 1941, a tremendous storm pushed the Gila River out of its banks and flooded the entire town of Duncan; houses constructed of mud bricks melted, and frame houses shifted on their foundations. Entire farms had almost disappeared, their crops swept away and their fields covered with gravel; a thousand sacks of onions floated downstream. Hundreds were homeless. Spencer helped transport relief supplies from the Church welfare storehouse in Safford to the flood victims, wading through swift water to survey the damage. As the water receded, he coordinated shoveling of mud out of homes and the heavy-equipment rehabilitation of farms. The experience proved the ability of the newly organized Church welfare program to provide substantial assistance in cases of local disasters.

On July 8, 1943, Spencer arrived home for lunch as the phone rang. The voice of President J. Reuben Clark, Jr., crackled across the phone lines. "Spencer, do you have a chair handy? The Brethren have just chosen you to fill one of the vacancies in the Quorum of the Twelve Apostles." Spencer protested that it couldn't be—that there must be some mistake—as he slid to the floor. President Clark reassured him. In an instant, every petty mistake, every misunderstanding, every wounded feeling raced through his mind. Voices seemed to ask, *How could you be an Apostle? You're not worthy. You can't do it.*

President Clark finally interrupted the silence. "Are you there?" Spencer knew there was only one answer, but asked if he could come to Salt Lake to discuss the call.

He would be giving up a business he had struggled to build for twenty-five years. He would be uprooting his family. He would be leaving behind life-long friends. He would be assuming responsibilities he felt incompetent to fill. But as he started to weep, he knew he had long ago committed to respond to any call from the Lord. As tears gave way to sobs, Camilla stroked his hair, trying to comfort him. "You can do it," she reassured him. "You can do anything the Lord asks of you."

He didn't sleep that night. In fact, he slept only fitfully throughout the next week, tossing restlessly in his bed.

On the way to Salt Lake City, Spencer and Camilla stopped in Colorado to visit LeVan and his family. Early in the morning, Spencer slipped out of the house; fasting, he began hiking straight up the mountain without waiting to find a path. He nearly stepped on a rattlesnake and jumped as it struck at him; he wondered if it were an omen. He wept as he climbed higher, alternately praying for confirmation from the Lord and mentally rehearsing his own weaknesses. He knew that someone had to be called; was it really the Lord's will that he be the one?

As he scrambled over rough rocks to the top of a cliff, he looked at the valley spread below him. It occurred to him that it would be easy to end his struggle by simply flinging himself off the rocks to the valley floor. He prayed as he had never prayed before—not for a vision, but for an answer. For a long time he wept and struggled. Finally, his answer came as in a dream he sensed his grandfather, Heber C. Kimball, and the great apostolic work he had done. He felt a tremendous calm. A great burden had been lifted, and he felt nearer to the Lord than ever before.

Arriving in Salt Lake City, he met with David O. McKay, a counselor in the First Presidency, to officially accept the call. Then he and Camilla returned to Arizona to pack up their lives and move to Utah.

At October general conference in 1943, the Church sustained Spencer W. Kimball and Ezra Taft Benson as Apostles. When President Heber J. Grant ordained Spencer, the admonition came to "make this cause and this labor first and foremost in all your thoughts." Spencer fully committed himself to that goal. At forty-eight, he started a new life.

While he was busy getting used to new responsibilities, the Church was busy getting acquainted with a new General Authority. At one of his first stake conferences, he was introduced as

Ezra Taft Benson. "That's all right with me," he told the congregation; "just don't tell Brother Benson!" After another meeting, a man shook his hand and said, "I'm so glad you came, Brother Richards; I always used to get you mixed up with Brother Lee."

In 1946, President George Albert Smith gave Elder Kimball a special assignment "to look after the Indians in all the world," a fulfillment of a promise in his patriarchal blessing that said, "You will preach the gospel to many people, but more especially to the Lamanites." He began traveling on the reservations, meeting and teaching, blessing the sick, and encouraging missionary work. At the time, missionaries could not rent, buy, or build on the reservations without permission, and it took several years of patient work before the tribal council would let Church members do more than just visit the reservation.

In 1947, a harsh early winter left many Navajos close to starvation. Elder Kimball created interest in their plight by writing newspaper and magazine articles, giving talks, and contacting service clubs. In response, the Church welfare system provided food and the Deseret News created an Indian Aid Caravan consisting of trucks that took food and warm clothing to the Indians, regardless of whether they were members of the Church. The Red Cross said of the incident that "one little man" had wakened the country—even motivating Congress to appropriate money to address the situation.

When Elder Kimball determined that the Indians needed better education in order to help solve their own problems, he oversaw development of the Indian Student Placement Program, which provided homes with sponsoring families for five thousand Indian children during the school year. The program continued until there were improved schools and roads on the reservations.

In 1955, President David O. McKay assigned Elder Kimball to visit all the missions in Europe, a task that took almost six months. Traveling through areas still rebuilding after the destruction of World War II, he and Camilla visited thirteen nations and encouraged the Saints to build the Church where they were. Elder Kimball told Church members that in spite of their poverty, they could find a way to go to the newly completed Swiss Temple. If they understood how important temple ordinances were, he told them, they would be willing to walk to Switzerland for those blessings.

In 1957, Elder Kimball's throat began to bother him seriously. For years he had experienced persistent hoarseness, but now his voice was weak and his throat occasionally bled.

When his throat failed to heal after a month of silence, a New York specialist, certain it was cancer, insisted on removing the entire voice box. When Elder Kimball explained the importance of his voice to his ministry, the surgeon agreed to leave half of one vocal cord to preserve the chance of some voice.

The four-inch incision on his neck became infected and took weeks to heal. The result was nothing more than a weak rasp—not a real voice—and he was reluctant to speak in public. When he was assigned to speak at a stake conference in Gila Valley, however, he decided he could not ask for a more understanding audience for his first effort. Addressing his friends, he said, "I went away to the East and fell among cutthroats and thieves. They slit my throat and stole my voice." The audience erupted in laughter, and Elder Kimball was grateful to be back at work. At the next general conference, he discovered that not only were people willing to listen to him, but they actually listened more carefully because of his unusual voice.

In 1965, Elder Kimball was assigned to supervise the missions in South America, which required traveling long distances over poor roads. He shoveled sand at a chapel construction site in Montevideo, set up chairs for conferences, and preached at an impromptu roadside gathering.

During his assignment in South America, he expanded missionary work to include millions of Indians living in the high valleys of the Andes Mountains—and he made certain they would be taught in their own languages.

Four years later he was assigned to supervise the missions in the British Isles. During his travels, he liked to give twelve-year-old boys a dollar—or its equivalent—for their missions. One friend gave him an entire box of silver dollars labeled "Seeds for the Spencer W. Kimball Missionary Garden." Subsequently he began giving dollars to girls, encouraging them to start a fund for traveling to the temple for their wedding.

In 1969, Spencer W. Kimball published *The Miracle of Forgiveness,* a book about the repentance process that later became a classic.

In 1970, Elder Kimball's throat cancer came back, and the surgeon wanted to remove the remaining piece of vocal cord. That wasn't all: Elder Kimball learned that his increasing fatigue was the result of a heart that was about to fail.

Though the surgeon had little regard for radiation treatment, Elder Kimball decided to try it, and after twenty-four cobalt treatments, the cancer was defeated. At that point, Dr. Russell M. Nelson—later to become a member of the Council of the Twelve—operated on Elder

Kimball's heart, putting in a mechanical valve and bypassing clogged arteries. Dr. Nelson later related that of the thousands of steps involved in the complicated surgery, not a single thing had gone wrong—and that he had been impressed that the man whose life he had just saved would one day preside over the Church.

The day after Christmas 1973, President Harold B. Lee suffered a sudden heart attack while in the hospital for a checkup and died. On Sunday, December 30, 1973, the Council of the Twelve—after seeking inspiration of the Lord—named Spencer Woolley Kimball twelfth president of the Church. He had been an Apostle for thirty years and was seventy-eight years old; in light of the serious health problems he had faced, many foresaw his administration as nothing more than a "caretaker" period. One little boy came to his office to shake his hand and stated frankly, "I wanted to see you before you died."

Nothing could have been farther from the truth. In April 1974, he addressed Regional Representatives about the importance of missionary work. He said the Lord would only open doors to nations when the Church was prepared to walk through them. With the now-famous charge to "lengthen our stride," the number of missionaries in the Church increased rapidly.

In 1975, Adney Y. Komatsu, called as an

Assistant to the Twelve, became the first non-Caucasian General Authority. In October of that year President Kimball organized the First Quorum of the Seventy; men representing half a dozen nations outside the United States were called to fill its ranks. Additional important administrative changes followed, including an emeritus status for elderly or ill General Authorities.

President Kimball encouraged the keeping of personal journals and the writing of family history, regarding genealogical research and the strengthening of family ties as part of religious obligation. He traveled the world speaking at area conferences and was instrumental in opening new nations for the preaching of the gospel. On June 9, 1978, he announced that the priesthood would be extended to every worthy male member of the Church, signaling the long-awaited opportunity for Blacks to hold the priesthood.

During the summer of 1979, his health began to fail. He suffered several small strokes, lost his sense of balance, and experienced fading eyesight. He soon needed assistance walking. A subdural hematoma (blood and fluid inside the skull) required emergency surgery. Defying all predictions, a few weeks later he delivered five talks at the October general conference. When his doctor urged him to slow down, he said, "My dear doctor, if you knew what I know about the timetable of the Lord, if you knew the commitments I have been required to make in the sacred office that I hold, you would find that there is no alternative."

By April general conference in 1981, despite a second surgery to relieve pressure on his brain, he reported that he had traveled 50,000 miles in the previous six months. Even with age and declining health, he encouraged a new edition of the standard works and saw that a new subtitle was added to the Book of Mormon—"Another Testament of Jesus Christ." A new Church museum took shape, and his open criticism of basing MX missiles in the Utah-Nevada desert caused President Ronald Reagan to refer the entire proposal back to the military for further study.

A reporter once asked him, "Do you ever worry about working too hard, killing yourself?" He replied, "A little, but not very much—not enough to stop."

His health and strength declined rapidly. He maintained, "My life is like my shoes, to be worn out in service." Through it all, his sense of humor stayed strong. When a nurse once asked him when the Second Coming would be, he asked, "Why? Are you ready?"

Despite his tired, worn-out body, he endured faithfully to the end, which came on November 5,

1985, at the age of ninety. He once observed, "I still wonder what the Lord was thinking about, making a little country boy like me President of His Church, unless He knew that I didn't have any sense and would just keep on working." No short man ever had a longer stride.

Excerpted with permission from *The Story of Spencer W. Kimball: A Short Man, A Long Stride* by Andrew E. Kimball, Jr., and Edward L. Kimball (Salt Lake City: Bookcraft, 1985).

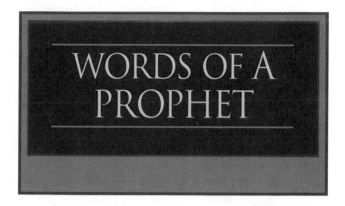

WORDS OF A PROPHET

ADVERSITY

It is the destiny of the spirits of men to come to this earth and travel a journey of indeterminate length. They travel sometimes dangerously, sometimes safely, sometimes sadly, sometimes happily. Always the road is marked by divine purpose. (*Miracle,* 1)

Being human, we would expel from our lives sorrow, distress, physical pain, and mental anguish and assure ourselves of continual ease and comfort. But if we closed the doors upon such, we might be evicting our greatest friends and benefactors. Suffering can make saints of people as they learn patience, long-suffering, and self-mastery. The sufferings of our Savior were part of His education. ("Tragedy or Destiny," *Improvement Era,* March 1966, 178)

Sometimes the solution is not to change our circumstance, but to change our attitude about that circumstance; difficulties are often opportunities for service. ("Small Acts of Service," *Ensign,* Dec. 1974, 2)

No pain suffered by man or woman upon the earth will be without its compensating effects if it be suffered in resignation and if it be met with patience. (Funeral of C. Rulon Harper, Pocatello, Idaho, April 1961)

AGENCY

Is it blind obedience when we with our limited vision, elementary knowledge, selfish desires, ulterior motives, and carnal urges, accept and follow the guidance and obey the commands of our loving Father who begot us, created a world for us, loves us, and has planned a constructive program for us, wholly without ulterior motive, whose greatest joy and glory is to "bring to pass the immortality and eternal life" of all His children?

Blind obedience it might be when no agency exists, when there is regimentation, but in all of the commands of the Lord given through His servants, there is total agency free of compulsion. Some remonstrate that agency is lacking where penalties are imposed and condemnations threatened—to be damned for rejecting the gospel seems harsh to some and to take away free agency. This is not true, for the decision is ours—we may accept or reject, comply or ignore. (*Faith,* 293)

We can satisfy ourselves with mediocrity. We can be common, ordinary, dull, colorless, or we can so channel our lives to be clean, vibrant, progressive, colorful, and rich.

We can soil our records, defile our souls, trample underfoot virtue, honor, and goodness, or we can command respect and admiration of our associates and the love of the Lord.

Your destiny is in your hands and your all-important decisions are before you. (Prepared for April 1972 General Conference)

The world would legislate goodness and make men fear to do wrong. The gospel would cause men to do right because it makes them happy to do right. ("The Gospel Solves Problems of the World," BYU 10-Stake Fireside, 26 Sept. 1971)

AGNOSTICISM

I believe agnosticism is a disease of youth and adulthood to which most are exposed and many suffer, but like other maladies, recovery is quite sure if known remedies are used. And a sure restorative is given by John when he said: "If any man will do his will, he shall know of the doctrine, whether it be of God, or whether I speak of myself." (John 7:17.) ("Spiritual Vision," BYU, 19 March 1946)

APPEARANCE

We are affected by our own outward appearances; we tend to fill roles. If we are in our Sunday best, we have little inclination for roughhousing; if we dress for work, we are drawn to work; if we dress immodestly, we are tempted to act immodestly; if we dress like the opposite sex, we tend to lose our sexual identity or some of the graces that distinguish the eternal mission of our sex.

Now, I hope not to be misunderstood: I am not saying that you should judge one another by appearance, for that would be folly and worse; I am saying that there is a relationship between how we dress and groom ourselves and how we are inclined to feel and act. ("Integrity: The Spirit of BYU," BYU, 4 Sept. 1979)

BAPTISM

All members have been baptized by immersion in water and have received the Holy Ghost by the laying on of hands by properly authorized men who hold the holy priesthood. We all have been received by baptism into The Church of Jesus Christ when we have humbled ourselves before God, have desired to be baptized, have come forth with broken hearts and contrite spirits, and when we have witnessed before the Church that we are truly repentant of our sins and are willing to take upon us the name of Jesus Christ, having a determination to serve Him to the end and thus manifest by our works that we have received the Spirit of Christ unto the remission of our sins. ("Why Call Me Lord, Lord, and Do Not the Things Which I Say?" *Ensign,* May 1975, 4)

BODY

All of us, even the child who dies in infancy, have received a body, which is an absolute necessity toward maximum growth and development. For the body, though disintegrated in death, will eventually be literally resurrected and our eternities will be spent in a body; but it will be one of flesh and bone and spirit, the corruptible blood being replaced by a finer substance giving life to the body. And thus, in this resurrected state, free from limitations of space and gravity and other forces to which we are subject here, our bodies, like that of the resurrected Redeemer, will be free to do much that the mortal body cannot do. (Utah State University, 25 Nov. 1958)

The body resurrected will be neither the unbalanced body of immature youth, nor the creaking, wrinkling one of many years, but when it is restored and resurrected it will undoubtedly return in the bloom of its greatest mortal perfection.

Some sectarian peoples minimize the body and look forward to freedom from it. Some flail and beat and torture the body, but the gospel of Jesus Christ magnifies the importance of the body and the dignity of man. This body will come forth in the resurrection. (Sermon, "The Spiritual Aspects of Body Preservation," undated)

BOOKS

Happy is the family whose members have learned to make good books their companions. The need of guidance by parents, teachers, and Church organizations is apparent, that the minds of children be properly stirred and fed. One is literally what he thinks, and his thinking is greatly influenced by what he reads. ("The Power of Books," *Relief Society Magazine,* Oct. 1963, 724)

Numerous people fail to take advantage of these opportunities. Many people spend hours in planes with only cursory glancing at magazines, and in the train or bus, time is spent "sitting and thinking," and in many cases, "just sitting," when there could be such a constructive program of reading. People in beauty parlors, professional offices, waiting rooms, and elsewhere waste precious hours thumbing through outdated magazines when much valuable reading could be done in these islands of time.

In addition to all the serious study there should be time for just plain reading for pleasure. Here one needs assistance to select that which is pleasurable in a worthwhile way. There are countless works of fiction which help us to understand ourselves and others better, and to get real pleasure in the learning. ("The Power of Books," *Relief Society Magazine,* Oct. 1963, 724)

CHANGE

First we make ourselves humble. We change our own lives; that is the beginning. We all want to change the nation in a day. A nation is made up of individuals. We start and change our own lives, and then we help another life to get the same ideals—and then there are two lives. And all the other individuals around us do the same thing; and here we have a community, and there another community; and several communities make a state and several states make a nation. And we can do it. The Lord will protect us. ("I Will Fight Your Battles," Kidderminster, England, July 1955)

CHARACTER

I stepped into the Hotel Utah coffee shop in Salt Lake City to buy some hard rolls, and as I placed my order with the waitress, a middle-aged woman I knew was sitting at the counter with a cup of coffee at her plate. I am sure she saw me, though she tried not to show it. I could see her physical discomfort as she turned her face from me at a right angle, and there it remained until I had made my purchase and had gone to the cash register. She had her free agency—she could drink coffee if she wanted to, but what a wallop her character had taken, because she was unwilling to face a friend! How she shriveled! (*Faith*, 241)

CHASTITY

None of us, I guess, are quite totally perfect. Perhaps there are thoughts that come into our minds. But that is the time to kill them and crush them and to put your heel on them and turn it to crush the thought that good could come from an adulterous thought. (Priesthood leadership meeting, Holbrook, Arizona, 20 Oct. 1974)

The problem of youth is to keep all urges and desires and passions properly harnessed and properly bridled. Nothing wrong with passion. The race would die out if it weren't for passion. But [passions] must be controlled. ("Immodesty in Dress," Portland Stake Conference, 9 Sept. 1956)

There are dark corners and hidden spots and closed cars in which the transgression can be committed, but to totally conceal it is impossible. There is no night so dark, no room so tightly locked, no canyon so closed in, no desert so totally uninhabited that one can find a place to hide from his sins, from himself, or from the Lord. Eventually, one must face the great Maker. (Copenhagen Area Conference, 5 Aug. 1976)

Uncontrolled passion can burn one into spiritual ashes. (*Youth,* 91)

CHILDREN

Many people in the Church do not have the right concept of a child. They think that he is a personality to play with, to dress, to enjoy, to have, to hold. They never think seriously about the tremendous responsibility of developing that little spirit without earthly knowledge into a fit subject for the kingdom of God. ("Those Precious, Early Years," Stake Junior Sunday School Coordinators, 5 April 1959)

We do not rear children just to please our vanity. We bring children into the world to become kings and queens, and priests and priestesses for our Lord. (Buenos Aires Area Conference, Parents' Meeting, 8 March 1975)

CHRIST

Christ is central to the gospel and the Church. The gospel of Jesus Christ knows no borders nor bounds. At the center of it all stands Jesus Christ, the resurrected Son of our Heavenly Father. ("The Family Is Forever," Baton Rouge, Louisiana, 15 May 1977)

We have a hope in Christ here and now. He died for our sins. Because of Him and His gospel, our sins are washed away in the waters of baptism; sin and iniquity are burned out of our souls as though by fire; and we become clean, have clear consciences, and gain that peace which passeth understanding. (See Philippians 4:7.)

But today is just a grain of sand in the Sahara of eternity. We have also a hope in Christ for the eternity that lies ahead; otherwise, as Paul said, we would be "of all men most miserable." (1 Corinthians 15:19.) ("An Eternal Hope in Christ," *Ensign,* Nov. 1978, 71)

We can see that not all activities we could engage in are of equal weight, even though they may appropriately be a part of a spiritually balanced family unity development program. Some concerns have higher priorities. We remember the words of Nephi as he counseled: "And we talk of Christ, we rejoice in Christ, we preach of Christ, we prophesy of Christ . . . that our children may know to what source they may look." (2 Nephi 25:26.) ("Therefore I Was Taught," *Ensign,* Jan. 1982, 3)

He was not an architect, nor a contractor, nor a builder. He was only a Galilean carpenter, a maker of wooden plows and oxen yokes. But He inspired the noblest, most marvelous architecture known to man. He himself specialized in character engineering, to make of men human master-pieces. He took a Peter and made a Saint. He took a Saul and made a Paul. And He took you and me and He will make of us gods if we will comply and follow along. What a picture! (Holbrook Arizona Seminary dedication, 10 May 1964)

Jesus Christ is the Son of God, the Almighty, the Creator, the Master of the only true way of life— the gospel of Jesus Christ. The intellectual may rationalize Him out of existence and the unbe-liever may scoff, but Christ still lives and guides the destinies of His people. That is an absolute truth; there is no gainsaying. ("Absolute Truth," *Ensign,* Sept. 1978, 3)

Both faith and works are needed for exaltation. There can be no real and true Christianity, even with good works, unless we are deeply and per-sonally committed to the reality of Jesus Christ as the Only Begotten Son of the Father, who bought us, who purchased us in the great act of atone-ment. ("The Savior: The Center of Our Lives," *New Era,* Apr. 1980, 33)

No matter how much we say of Him, it is still too little. He is not only the Carpenter, the Nazarene, the Galilean, but Jesus Christ, the God of this earth, the Son of God, but most importantly, our Savior, our Redeemer. ("Integrity," Salt Lake Rotary Club, 17 Dec. 1974)

Declare allegiance to Christ. It is not enough to refrain from profanity or blasphemy. We need to make important in our lives the name of the Lord Jesus Christ. In the waters of baptism we take upon us the name of Christ. And as we partake of the sacrament of the Lord's Supper, we renew that commitment. While we do not use the Lord's name lightly, we should not leave our friends and our neighbors or our children in any doubt where we stand. (Independence Missouri Stake Center dedication, 3 Sept. 1978)

Sometimes an individual stands alone in a family as a witness for Christ. God bless him who stands faithful and true, even alone. (Stockholm Area Conference, 18 Aug. 1974)

To be like Christ! What an ambitious goal! What a lofty ideal! The Savior had a pleasing personality, He was kind, He was pleasant, He was understanding, He never went off on tangents, He was perfectly balanced. No eccentricities could be found in His life. Here was no ostentation and show, but He was real and humble and genuine.

He made no play for popularity. He made no compromises to gain favor. He did the right thing always, regardless of how it might appeal to men. He drew all good people to Him as a magnet. "What manner of men ought ye to be?" The answer, "Even as I am." ("What Manner of Men Ought Ye to Be," Jordan Seminary graduation, 14 May 1954)

CHRISTMAS

Christmas comes to remind us of the fatherhood of God and the brotherhood of man. It comes to show us the real progress we would make, could all our days be unselfish, friendly, helpful, and clear of bitterness and strife. (St. Joseph Stake Primary, Thatcher, Arizona, 16 Dec. 1934)

CHURCH

We are impressed that the mission of the Church is threefold:

- To proclaim the gospel of the Lord Jesus Christ to every nation, kindred, tongue, and people;
- To perfect the Saints by preparing them to receive the ordinances of the gospel and by

instruction and discipline to gain exaltation;
- To redeem the dead by performing vicarious ordinances of the gospel for those who have lived on the earth.

All three are part of one work—to assist our Father in Heaven and his Son, Jesus Christ, in their grand and glorious mission "to bring to pass the immortality and eternal life of man." (Moses 1:39.) ("A Report of My Stewardship," *Ensign,* May 1981, 5)

The basic decisions needed for us to move forward, as a people, must be made by the individual members of the Church. The major strides which must be made by the Church will follow upon the major strides to be made by us as individuals. ("A Report of My Stewardship," *Ensign,* May 1981, 5)

This is not *A* church; it is *The* Church of Jesus Christ. There are churches of men all over the land and they have great cathedrals, synagogues, and other houses of worship running into the hundreds of millions of dollars. They are the churches of men. They teach the doctrines of men, combined with the philosophies and ethics and other ideas and ideals that men have partly developed and partly found in sacred places and interpreted for themselves. But there is just one church which Jesus Christ, Himself, organized by direct revelation; just one church that teaches all of His doctrines; just one church which has all of the keys and authorities which are necessary to carry on the work of Jesus Christ. (New York Stake Conference, 23 Feb. 1957)

CHURCH GOVERNMENT

The moment life passes from a President of the Church, a body of men become the composite leader—these men already seasoned with experience and training. The appointments have long been made, the authority given, the keys delivered. . . . The kingdom moves forward under this already authorized council. No "running" for position, no electioneering, no stump speeches. What a divine plan! How wise our Lord, to organize so perfectly beyond the weakness of frail, grasping humans.

Then dawns the notable day . . . and fourteen serious men walk reverently into the temple of God—this is the Quorum of the Twelve Apostles, the governing body of The Church of Jesus Christ of Latter-day Saints, several of whom have experienced this solemn change before.

When these fourteen men emerge from the holy edifice later in the morning, a transcendently vital event has occurred—a short interregnum ends, and the government of the kingdom shifts back again from the Quorum of the Twelve Apostles to a new prophet, an individual leader, the Lord's earthly representative. ("The Need for a Prophet," *Improvement Era,* June 1970, 92)

Since the death of His servants is in the power and control of the Lord, He permits to come to the first place only the one who is destined to take that leadership. Death and life become the controlling factors. Each new Apostle in turn is chosen by the Lord and revealed to the then living prophet who ordains him. ("We Thank Thee, O God, for a Prophet," *Ensign,* Jan. 1973, 33)

We may expect the Church President will always be an older man; young men have action, vigor, initiative; older men, stability and strength and wisdom through experience and long communion with God. . . .

What the world needs is a prophet-leader who gives example—clean, full of faith, godlike in his attitudes, with an untarnished name, a beloved husband, a true father. . . .

I make no claim of infallibility for him, but he does need to be recognized of God as an authoritative person.

He must be bold enough to speak truth even against popular clamor for lessening restrictions. He must be certain of his divine appointment, of his celestial ordination, and his authority to call to service, to ordain, to pass keys which fit eternal locks. ("The Need for a Prophet," *Improvement Era,* June 1970, 92)

CHURCH PROGRAMS

People are more important than programs, and Church programs should always support and never detract from gospel-centered family activities. ("Living the Gospel in the Home," *Ensign,* May 1978, 100)

CONSCIENCE

Conscience tells the individual when he is entering forbidden worlds, and it continues to prick until silenced by the will or by sin's repetition. ("President Kimball Speaks Out on Morality," *Ensign,* Nov. 1980, 94)

When a person pushes the Spirit away and ignores and puts out the "unwelcome sign," eventually the Spirit of the Lord ceases to strive. He does not move away from the individual; it is the person who moves away from the Lord. ("New Horizons for Homosexuals," pamphlet)

You must realize that you have something like the compass, like the Liahona, in your own system. Every child is given it. When he is eight years of age, he knows good from evil, if his parents have been teaching him well. If he ignores the Liahona that he has in his own makeup, he eventually may not have it whispering to him. But if we will remember that every one of us has the thing that will direct him aright, our ship will not get on the wrong course . . . if we listen to the dictates of our own Liahona, which we call the conscience. ("Our Own Liahona," *Ensign,* Nov. 1976, 77)

COURTSHIP

Youth should emphasize group social activities. The urge for group activity is normal to the younger set, when they are not prematurely and immaturely stimulated in other ways, and the recreational and social activities of the crowd can be wholesome and entertaining.

Physical and moral safety is increased in the multiplicity of friends. Group homemade recreation activities can be not only great fun but most beneficial. Firesides may create friendships, and inspire the spirit and train the mind. Group picnics can discipline youth in gentle manners and fellowship and extend circles of intimate friends.

Sports can develop the body in strength and endurance. They can train the spirit to meet difficulties and defeats and successes, teach selflessness and understanding, and develop good sportsmanship and tolerance in participant and spectator. Drama can develop talent, teach patience, and foster fellowship and friendliness. Group music activities have similar effects, and also can soften and mellow the spirit and satisfy the aesthetic needs.

The properly conducted dancing party can be a blessing. It provides opportunity to spend a pleasant evening with many people to the accompaniment of music. It can create and develop friendships which will be treasured in later years. (*Miracle*, 221–22)

CREATION

Man is the masterpiece—in all the creations of God nothing even approaches him. The animals were given instincts. They can seize food, escape from enemies, hide from danger, sleep and rest, but they have practically none of the faculties given to this god-man, to this god in embryo. (Funeral of Orley Glenn Stapley, Phoenix, Arizona, 1948)

God made man in his own image and certainly He made woman in the image of His wife-partner. ("Permissiveness," Ricks College, 28 March 1972)

DEATH

I am positive in my mind that the Lord has planned our destiny. We can shorten our lives, but I think we cannot lengthen them very much. Sometime we'll understand fully, and when we see back from the vantage point of the future, we shall be satisfied with many of the happenings of this life which seemed so difficult for us to comprehend. ("Tragedy or Destiny," *Improvement Era,* March 1966, 178)

If mortality be the perfect state, then death would be a frustration, but the gospel teaches us there is no tragedy in death, but only in sin.

We know so little; *our* judgment is so limited. We judge the Lord often with less wisdom than does our youngest child weigh our decisions. ("Tragedy or Destiny," *Improvement Era,* March 1966, 178)

In death do we grieve for the one who passes on, or is it self-pity? To doubt the wisdom and justice of the passing of a loved one is to place a limitation on the term of life. It is to say that it is more important to continue to live here than to go into other fields. Do we grieve when our son is graduated from the local high school and is sent away from home to a university of higher learning? Do we grieve inconsolably when our son is called away from our daily embrace to distant lands to preach the gospel? To continue to grieve without faith and understanding and trust when a son goes into another world is to question the long-range program of God, life eternal with all its opportunities and blessings. ("Thy Son Liveth," *Improvement Era,* May 1945, 253)

Though death is more common during war, death's meaning is the same. To the unbeliever it is the end of all, associations terminated, relationships ended, memories soon to fade into nothingness. (Funeral of Janie Pace, Safford, Arizona, 1943)

Every promise of God will be fulfilled. A virtuous, progressive, active young man will sacrifice no blessing to which he was entitled by his (to us) premature passing into eternity. We may not understand fully just how it will be accomplished, but we may know that it will be. Remember what the Lord Himself said: "Eye hath not seen, nor ear heard, neither have entered into the heart of man, the things which God hath prepared for them that love him." (1 Corinthians 2:9.)

Can we not trust in the goodness of the Lord? Remember that He is the Father also of this son. He is the Parent of the living part, you of the tabernacle only. Will He not be infinitely more concerned with the welfare of this son than we mortals could ever be? Can we not know this: "His purposes fail not, neither are there any who can stay his hand"? (D&C 76:3.) ("The Sabbath Day," *Improvement Era,* May 1944, 285)

DECISIONS

Right decisions are easiest to make when we make them well in advance, having ultimate objectives in mind; this saves a lot of anguish at the fork, when we're tired and sorely tempted.

Some people feel that decisions are really out of our hands, that we merely respond to circumstances without choice, like a rudderless ship that drifts at the mercy of the wind and waves. And I agree that there can come a time when we no longer have control over our destinies, but I believe that this is only after the cumulation of our own past decisions has left us helpless. ("Decisions: Why It's Important to Make Some Now," *New Era,* April 1971, 2)

DETERMINATION

No one should deny the importance of circumstances, yet in the final analysis the most important thing is how we react to the circumstances.

I have seen poverty produce quite different results in people; some it embitters, so that in their self-pity they simply give up and abandon the future; others it challenges, so that in their determination to succeed in spite of obstacles they grow into capable, powerful people. Even if they never escape from economic stress, they develop inner resources that we associate with progress toward a Christlike character. ("Decisions: Why It's Important to Make Some Now," *New Era*, April 1971, 2)

Wanted! Youth who will maturely carve their own destinies from the hard marble of life with the chisels of courage and mallets of determination and undeviating purpose. (*Youth*, 73)

DILIGENCE

The "lengthening of our stride" suggests urgency instead of hesitancy, "now" instead of tomorrow; it suggests not only an acceleration, but efficiency. It suggests, too, that the whole body of the

Church move forward in unison with a quickened pace and pulse, doing our duty with all our heart, instead of halfheartedly. It means, therefore, mobilizing and stretching all our muscles and drawing on all our resources. It suggests also that we stride with pride and with a sense of anticipation as we meet the challenges facing the kingdom. Out of all this will come a momentum that will be sobering and exhilarating at the same time. . . . The idea of "lengthening our stride" or "stretching our muscles" or "reaching our highest" has an interesting scriptural base. The second verse in the fifty-fourth chapter of Isaiah proclaims: "Enlarge the place of thy tent, and let them stretch forth the curtains of thine habitations: spare not, lengthen thy cords, and strengthen thy stakes." (MIA June Conference, 29 June 1975)

DISCIPLINE

The sad, simple truth is that when we do not act preventively, we must, later on, act redemptively. ("Lengthening Our Stride," Regional Representatives Conference, 3 Oct. 1974)

DIVORCE

Those who claim their love is dead should return home with all their loyalty, fidelity, honor, cleanliness—and the love which has become embers will flare up with scintillating flame again. If love wanes or dies, it is often infidelity of thought or act which gave the lethal potion. I plead with all people, young and old, bound by marriage vows and covenants to make that marriage holy, keep it fresh, express affection meaningfully and sincerely and often. Thus will one avoid the pitfalls which destroy marriages. (*Miracle*, 251)

DOUBT

Even to the religionist there may come a day of doubt and misgivings, but with patience most will plod through this period of adjustment and emerge from the darkness strengthened and reassured in the faith. (Ft. Thomas High School baccalaureate, 14 May 1963)

EDUCATION

We understand, as few people do, that education is a part of being about our Father's business and that the scriptures contain the master concepts for mankind. (Ft. Thomas High School baccalaureate, 14 May 1963)

ENHANCING LIFE

It is not enough to refrain from killing. We are rather under the obligation to respect life and to foster it. Far from killing, we must be generous in helping others to have the necessities of life. We must find ways to help them to have a more abundant life, satisfying life, beyond mere existence. And when these have been accomplished, we seek to foster the life of the mind and the spirit. (Independence Missouri Stake Center dedication, 3 Sept. 1978)

ENVIRONMENT

You can change by changing your environment. Let go of lower things, and reach for higher. Surround yourself with the best in books, music, art, and people. ("Small Acts of Service," *Ensign,* Dec. 1974, 2)

We are concerned when we see numerous front and side and back yards that have gone to weeds, where ditch banks are cluttered and trash and refuse accumulate. It grieves us when we see broken fences, falling barns, leaning and unpainted sheds, hanging gates, and unpainted property. We ask our people again to take stock of their own dwellings and properties. ("Why Call Me Lord, Lord, and Do Not the Things Which I Say?" *Ensign,* May 1975, 4)

ETERNAL MARRIAGE

Any of you would go around the world for the sealing ordinance if you knew its importance, if you realized how great it is. No distance, no shortage of funds, no situation would ever keep you from being married in the holy temple of the Lord. ("The Matter of Marriage," University of Utah Institute of Religion, 22 Oct. 1976)

The greatest joys of true married life can be continued. The most beautiful relationships of parents and children can be made permanent. The holy association of families can be never-ending if husband and wife have been sealed in the holy bond of eternal matrimony. Their joys and progress will never end, but this will never fall into place of its own accord. ("Be Ye Therefore Perfect," BYU, 17 Sept. 1974)

EXALTATION

You could be the queen of Holland, the czar of Russia, or the emperor of Japan. You could be any great person in this world, but you would be a pygmy compared to what you can be in this Church. Every one of you can be a queen who will not lose her crown when she dies, a king who will not lose his sceptre when he dies. Every one of you! Not just the smartest of you, but every one of you can become a queen or a king and have princes and princesses of your own. It all depends on what you do. (Lamanite Conference, San Diego, California, 3 May 1975)

EXCELLENCE

One of the rich rewards coming from doing great things is the capacity to do still greater things. ("Education for Eternity," BYU, 12 Sept. 1967)

FAITH

Security is not born of inexhaustible wealth but of unquenchable faith. And generally that kind of faith is born and nurtured in the home and in childhood. ("The Family Influence," *Ensign*, July 1973, 15)

In faith we plant the seed, and soon we see the miracle of the blossoming. Men have often misunderstood and have reversed the process. They would have the harvest before the planting, the reward before the service, the miracle before the faith. Even the most demanding labor unions would hardly ask the wages before the labor. But many of us would have the vigor without the observance of the health laws, prosperity through the opened windows of heaven without the payment of our tithes. We would have the close communion with our Father without fasting and praying; we would have rain in due season and peace in the land without observing the Sabbath and keeping the other commandments of the Lord. We would pluck the rose before planting the roots; we would harvest the grain before sowing and cultivating. . . .

Know this, that just as undaunted faith has stopped the mouths of lions, made ineffective fiery flames, opened dry corridors through rivers and seas, protected against deluge and drought, and brought heavenly manifestations at the instance of prophets, so in each of our lives faith can heal the sick, bring comfort to those who mourn, strengthen resolve against temptation, relieve from the bondage of harmful habits, lend the strength to repent and change our lives, and lead to a sure knowledge of the divinity of Jesus

Christ. Indomitable faith can help us live the commandments with a willing heart and thereby bring blessings unnumbered, with peace, perfection, and exaltation in the kingdom of God. (*Faith,* 11–12)

Many people are administered to and are not healed. That is true, as it has been in all times. It was never intended that all should be healed or that all should be raised from the dead, else the whole program of mortality and death and resurrection and exaltation would be frustrated.

However, the Lord does make specific promises: Signs will follow them that believe. He makes no promise that signs will create belief nor save nor exalt. Signs are the product of faith. They are born in the soil of unwavering sureness. They will be prevalent in the Church in about the same degree to which the people have true faith. ("The Significance of Miracles in the Church Today," *Instructor,* Dec. 1959, 396)

Adam was a man of God with a great faith, and he continued to offer sacrifices unto the Lord because it had been commanded, even though he did not fully understand why, and even though it meant a considerable financial sacrifice to him. Why did he offer sacrifices?—because it was a commandment of his Heavenly Father. He had been told to perform this act by one whom he knew to be his God. He had absolute faith and confidence that blessings would come through such obedience, and he did not hesitate. After he had lived the law, then came the understanding, for the miracle follows the faith rather than faith the miracle. The angel explained to him that it was to keep him in constant memory of the coming of the Christ who would save the world, and exalt those of the people who would live the commandments. ("The Spirit Giveth Life," *Improvement Era,* Dec. 1951, 899)

FAMILY

It is important for us to cultivate in our own family a sense that we belong together eternally, that whatever changes outside our home, there are fundamental aspects of our relationship which will never change. We ought to encourage our children to know their relatives. We need to talk of them, make effort to correspond with them, visit them, join family organizations, etc. ("Ocean Currents and Family Influences," *Ensign,* Nov. 1974, 110)

The icebergs spawned by the Greenland ice sheet follow a highly predictable course. As the silent Labrador Current ceaselessly moves to the south through Baffin Bay and Davis Strait, it takes with it these mountainous icebergs, even against the force of the winds and the waves and the tides. Currents have much more power to control their course than the surface winds.

The current of our life, as defined and developed in the lives of a family by the righteous teaching of parents, will often control the direction children will go, in spite of the waves and winds of numerous adverse influences of the world of error.

I have sometimes seen children of good families rebel, resist, stray, sin, and even actually fight God. In this they bring sorrow to their parents, who have done their best to set in movement a current and to teach and live as examples. But I have repeatedly seen many of these same children, after years of wandering, mellow, realize what they have been missing, repent, and make great contribution to the spiritual life of their community. The reason I believe this can take place is that, despite all the adverse winds to which these people have been subjected, they have been influenced still more, and much more than they realized, by the current of life in the homes in which they were reared. When, in later years, they feel a longing to recreate in their own families the same atmosphere they enjoyed as children, they are likely to turn to the faith that gave meaning to their parents' lives.

There is no guarantee, of course, that righteous parents will succeed always in holding their children, and certainly they may lose them if they do not do all in their power. The children have their free agency.

But if we as parents fail to influence our families and set them on the "strait and narrow way," then certainly the waves, the winds of temptation and evil will carry the posterity away from the path. . . . What we do know is that righteous parents who strive to develop wholesome influences for their children will be held blameless at the last day, and that they will succeed in saving most of their children, if not all. ("Ocean Currents and Family Influences," *Ensign*, Nov. 1974, 110)

Motherhood and fatherhood are primary. Now, it is wise for every young woman to be grateful for her womanhood and her privilege to create, with her husband and the Eternal God as her partners. To be a mother, to be a wife of a good man—what a great joy! While she is waiting for that holy, sacred hour, let her be happy and content to develop her mind and accumulate knowledge and prepare herself emotionally and spiritually for the happy times.

For the young man, his education is important, his mission vital; but his proper marriage and his proper life to be a righteous father and to properly provide for and give leadership to a family—that is wonderful, a wonderful role in life to play. ("Be Ye Therefore Perfect," BYU, 17 Sept. 1974)

How long has it been since you took your children, whatever their size, in your arms and told them that you love them and are glad that they can be yours forever? How long has it been since you husbands or wives purchased an inexpensive gift as a surprise for your spouse for no other reason than just to please? How long has it been since you brought home a rose or baked a pie with a heart carved in the crust or did some other thing to make life more aglow with warmth and affection? ("Ocean Currents and Family Influences," *Ensign,* Nov. 1974, 110)

If there is to be a contribution to the building fund or the Red Cross, or a Saturday morning spent helping the elders quorum paint a widow's house, make sure the children are aware of it, and if it is feasible, let them have a share in the decision making and in the implementation of the decision. All the family could attend the baptism, confirmation, and ordination of a member of the family. All of the family could root for a son who is on the ball team. All meet regularly in home evening, at mealtime, at prayer time. Perhaps all of the family could pay tithing together, and each learns by precept and example the beautiful principle. ("Home

Training—The Cure for Evil," *Improvement Era,*
June 1965, 512)

To any thoughtful person it must be obvious that
intimate association without marriage is sin; that
children without parents and family life is tragedy;
that society without basic family life is without
foundation and will disintegrate into nothingness
and oblivion. ("The Family Influence," *Ensign,*
July 1973, 15)

FAMILY HOME EVENING

The gospel has been a family affair. By committing
ourselves to having the regular and inspirational
family home evening and by carefully planning the
content of that evening, we are sending a signal to
our children which they will remember forever-
more. When thus we give our children of our own
time, we are giving of our presence, a gift that is
always noticed. ("The True Way of Life and
Salvation," *Ensign,* May 1978, 4)

FAST OFFERING

Sometimes we have been a bit penurious and fig-
ured that we had for breakfast one egg and that

cost so many cents and then we give that to the Lord. I think that when we are affluent, as many of us are, that we ought to be very, very generous. I think we should . . . give, instead of the amount saved by our two meals of fasting, perhaps much, much more—ten times more when we are in a position to do it. (Conference Report, April 1974, 184)

FASTING

Failing to fast is a sin. In the fifty-eighth chapter of Isaiah, rich promises are made by the Lord to those who fast and assist the needy. Freedom from frustrations, freedom from thralldom, and the blessing of peace are promised. Inspiration and spiritual guidance will come with righteousness and closeness to our Heavenly Father. To omit this righteous act of fasting would deprive us of these blessings. (*Miracle,* 98)

Upon practicing the law of the fast, one finds a personal wellspring of power to overcome self-indulgence and selfishness. ("Becoming the Pure in Heart," *Ensign,* May 1978, 79)

We often have our individual reasons for fasting. But I hope members won't hesitate to fast to help us lengthen our stride in our missionary effort, to open the way for the gospel to go to the nations where it is not now permitted. It's good for us to fast as well as to pray over specific things and over specific objectives. ("Family Preparedness," *Ensign,* May 1976, 124)

FATHER'S BLESSING

A child leaving to go away to school or on a mission, a wife suffering stress, a family member being married or desiring guidance in making an important decision—all these are situations in which the father, in exercise of his patriarchal responsibility, can bless his family. ("Ocean Currents and Family Influences," *Ensign,* Nov. 1974, 110)

FORGIVENESS

The offended person should take the initiative. It frequently happens that offenses are committed when the offender is not aware of it. Something he has said or done is misconstrued or misunderstood. The offended one treasures in his heart the offense, adding to it such other things as might give fuel to the fire and justify his conclusions.

Perhaps this is one of the reasons why the Lord requires that the offended one should make the overtures toward peace. ("'Except Ye Repent,'" *Improvement Era,* Nov. 1949, 712)

I was struggling with a community problem in a small ward . . . where two prominent men, leaders of the people, were deadlocked in a long and unrelenting feud. Some misunderstanding between them had driven them far apart with enmity. As the days, weeks, and months passed, the breach became wider. The families of each conflicting party began to take up the issue and finally nearly all the people of the ward were involved. Rumors spread and differences were aired and gossip became tongues of fire until the little community was divided by a deep gulf. I was sent to clear up the matter. After a long stake conference, lasting most of two days, I arrived at the frustrated community about six p.m. Sunday night, and immediately went into session with the principal combatants.

How we struggled! How I pleaded and warned and begged and urged! Nothing seemed to be moving them. Each antagonist was so sure that he was right and justified that it was impossible to budge them.

The hours were passing—it was now long after midnight, and despair seemed to enshroud the place; the atmosphere was still one of ill temper and ugliness. Stubborn resistance would not give way. Then it happened. I aimlessly opened my Doctrine and Covenants again and there before me it was. I had read it many times in past years and it had had no special meaning then. But tonight it was the very answer. It was an appeal and an imploring and a threat and seemed to be coming direct from the Lord. I read from the seventh verse on, but the quarreling participants yielded not an inch until I came to the ninth verse. Then I saw them flinch, startled, wondering. Could that be right? The Lord was saying to us—to all of us—"Wherefore, I say unto you, that ye ought to forgive one another."

This was an obligation. They had heard it before. They had said it in repeating the Lord's Prayer. But now: ". . . for he that forgiveth not his brother his trespasses standeth condemned before the Lord. . . ." (D&C 64:7–9.)

In their hearts, they may have been saying: "Well, I might forgive if he repents and asks forgiveness, but he must make the first move." Then the full impact of the last line seemed to strike them: "For there remaineth in him the greater sin."

What? Does that mean I must forgive even if my antagonist remains cold and indifferent and mean? There is no mistaking it.

A common error is the idea that the offender must apologize and humble himself to the dust before forgiveness is required. Certainly, the one who does the injury should totally make his adjustment, but as for the offended one, he must forgive the offender regardless of the attitude of the other. Sometimes men get satisfaction from seeing the other party on his knees and groveling in the dust, but that is not the gospel way.

Shocked, the two men sat up, listened, pondered a minute, then began to yield. This scripture added to all the others read brought them to their knees. Two a.m. and two bitter adversaries were shaking hands, smiling and forgiving and asking forgiveness. Two men were in a meaningful embrace. This hour was holy. Old grievances were forgiven and forgotten, and enemies became friends again. (*Miracle,* 281–82)

One day in the temple in Salt Lake City, as I walked down the long hall preparing to go into one of the rooms to perform a marriage for a young couple, a woman followed me . . . and with great agitation she said, "Elder Kimball, do you remember me?" Her eyes were searching and her ears were seeking to hear if I remembered her. I was abashed. For the life of me I could not make the connection. I was much embarrassed. I finally said, "I am sorry, but I cannot remember you."

Instead of disappointment, there was great joy that came to her face. She was relieved. She said, "Oh, I am so grateful you can't remember me. With my husband I spent all night with you one time, while you were trying to change our lives. We had committed sin, and we were struggling to get rid of it. You labored all night to help me to clear it. We have repented, and we have changed our lives totally. I am glad you don't remember me, because if you, one of the Apostles, cannot remember me, maybe the Savior cannot remember my sins." (Amsterdam Area Conference, 7 Aug. 1976)

When we think of miracles, most of us think of healings under the power of the priesthood. But there is another, even greater miracle—the miracle of forgiveness.

The essence of the miracle of forgiveness is that it brings peace to the previously anxious, restless, frustrated, perhaps tormented soul. In a world of turmoil and contention this is indeed a priceless gift. (*Miracle,* 362–63)

FREEDOM

It is a strange thing when you stop to think about it. The road to this land of the United States is pretty nearly a one-way street. Everyone wants to come here. Nobody wants to leave. You probably never knew anyone who wanted to give up his American citizenship.

Why is this so? Is it because we have more to eat? Better homes? Better living conditions? That cannot be, because people wanted to come here when this was a country of hardship.

No, it is not just dollars. The early pioneers could have told you what it was. It is freedom. It is personal liberty. It is all of the human rights that millions of Americans have died for.

The sad part of it is that a lot of us take our civil rights for granted. We were born in a free country. We think freedom could never end. But it could. It is ending today in many countries. We could lose it, too. ("The Winning of the West," Salt Lake Rotary Club, 8 June 1976)

FRIENDSHIP

Friendships are not on the bargain counter; love is not on the market. Peace of mind, joy, and happiness cannot be purchased with money or worldly goods. ("The Abundant Life," Safford High School commencement, Safford, Arizona, 1939)

Never waste an hour with anyone who doesn't lift you up and encourage you. (Dortmund Area Conference, 8 Aug. 1976)

GARDENS

Many have done much to beautify their homes and their yards. Many others have followed the counsel to have their own gardens wherever it is possible so that we do not lose contact with the soil and so that we can have the security of being able to provide at least some of our food and necessities. ("The True Way of Life and Salvation," *Ensign,* May 1978, 4)

GATHERING

Now, the gathering of Israel consists of joining the true church and their coming to a knowledge of the true God. Any person, therefore, who has accepted the restored gospel, and who now seeks to worship the Lord in his own tongue and with the Saints in the nations where he lives, has complied with the law of the gathering of Israel and is heir to all of the blessings promised the Saints in these last days. ("The Gathering of Israel," Honolulu Area Conference, 18 June 1978)

GENERAL CONFERENCE

As we return to our homes, brothers and sisters, I hope we will not close the door on the conference.

Take it with us. Take it home with us. Tell our families about it, perhaps some to report in sacrament meetings of it. But take it to your families and give them the benefit of any inspiration that might have come to you, any determinations to change your lives and make them more acceptable to your Heavenly Father. ("Ocean Currents and Family Influences," *Ensign,* Nov. 1974, 110)

GOD

God, our Heavenly Father—Elohim—lives. That is an absolute truth. All four billion of the children of men on the earth might be ignorant of Him and His attributes and His powers, but He still lives. All the people on the earth might deny Him and disbelieve, but He lives in spite of them. They may have their own opinions, but He still lives, and His form, powers, and attributes do not change according to men's opinions. In short, opinion alone has no power in the matter of an absolute truth. He still lives. ("Absolute Truth," *Ensign,* Sept. 1978, 3)

Basic things have not changed since Adam. Men still have the same inherent goodnesses and weaknesses. Passions, urges, desires, wants are unchanged. Sin has not changed. Right has not changed. God has not changed. (BYU graduation, 22 Aug. 1963)

GODHEAD

There are three Gods: the Eternal Father, Elohim, to whom we pray; Christ or Jehovah; and the Holy Ghost who testifies of the others and witnesses to us the truth of all things. ("'For They Shall See God,'" *Improvement Era,* June 1964, 496)

GOSPEL

The gospel is true beyond all questioning. There may be parts of it we do not yet know and fully understand, but we shall never be able to prove it untrue for it includes all truth, known and unknown, developed and undeveloped. ("Permissiveness," Ricks College, 28 March 1972)

We endeavor to convince the world that where the truths of man-made organizations end, the gospel of Jesus Christ continues. The truths they teach are largely ethical. We go forward from there with ethics and gospel that carries us through the mortal life and on past the heaven of their fondest dreams into worlds of progression and creative work which are to their religious concepts as the airplane to the bumblebee. (Letter dated 6 March 1947)

HAPPINESS

And when we are asked why we are such a happy people, our answer is: "Because we have every-thing—life with all its opportunities, death without fear, eternal life with endless growth and develop-ment." ("God Will Not Be Mocked," *Ensign,* Nov. 1974, 4)

HEALING

It must be remembered that no physician can heal. He can only provide a satisfactory environment and situation so that the body may use its own God-given power of re-creation to build itself. Bones can be straightened, germs can be killed, sutures can close wounds and skillful fingers can open and close bodies; but no man yet has found a way to actually heal. Man is the offspring of God and has within him the re-creating power that is God-given. And through the priesthood and through prayer, the body's healing processes can be speeded and encouraged. (*Speaks,* 79)

We are assured by the Lord that the sick will be healed if the ordinance is performed, if there is sufficient faith, and if the ill one is "not appointed unto death." (D&C 42:48.) Here are three factors. Many do not comply with the ordinances, and great numbers are unwilling or incapable of exercising sufficient faith. But there is the other factor which looms important: if they are not appointed unto death. Every act of God is purposeful. He sees the end from the beginning. He knows what will build us, or tear us down, and what will thwart the program and what will give us eventual triumph. ("Tragedy or Destiny," *Improvement Era,* March 1966, 178)

Would you dare to take the responsibility of bringing back to life your own loved ones? I, myself, would hesitate to do so. I am grateful that we may always pray: "Thy will be done in all things, for thou knowest what is best." ("Tragedy or Destiny," *Improvement Era,* March 1966, 178)

HEALTH

[Physical fitness] is a part of the program—that we will perfect our physical bodies. We will make them just as attractive as possible. We will keep them as healthy as possible. We will keep them in the best condition we can. And so, we will make them like our Lord's. But, the most important thing is to gear our minds and our spirits so they will be like the Savior's. (Holbrook Arizona Seminary dedication, 10 May 1964)

HEAVENLY MOTHER

When we sing that doctrinal hymn and anthem of affection, "O My Father," we get a sense of the ultimate in maternal modesty, of the restrained, queenly elegance of our Heavenly Mother, and knowing how profoundly our mortal mothers have shaped us here, do we suppose Her influence on us as individuals to be less if we live so as to return there? ("The True Way of Life and Salvation," *Ensign,* May 1978, 4)

HOLY GHOST

The Holy Ghost is a personage of spirit and comes into our lives to lead us in the paths of righteousness. Each person on whom authoritative hands have been placed will receive the Holy Ghost. He will lead us unto all truth. And so we are a blessed people with all these special blessings. If one does not receive the great gift of the

Holy Ghost, then it is his fault that he hasn't been spiritual enough or close enough to Heavenly Father. (Seoul Area Conference, 17 Aug. 1975)

The Holy Ghost is a revelator. Every worthy soul is entitled to a revelation, and it comes through the Holy Ghost. In Moroni's farewell to the Lamanites, he says: "And by the power of the Holy Ghost ye may know the truth of all things." (Moroni 10:5.)

He is a reminder and will bring to our remembrance the things which we have learned and which we need in the time thereof. He is an inspirer and will put words in our mouths, enlighten our understandings and direct our thoughts. He is a testifier and will bear record to us of the divinity of the Father and the Son and of their missions and of the program which they have given us. He is a teacher and will increase our knowledge. He is a companion and will walk with us, inspiring us all along the way, guiding our footsteps, impeaching our weaknesses, strengthening our resolves, and revealing to us righteous aims and purposes. ("The Fourth Article of Faith," *Instructor,* April 1955, 108)

The missionary does not convert anyone: the Holy Ghost does the converting. The power of conversion is directly associated with the Holy Ghost, for no person can be truly converted and know that Jesus is the Christ save by the power of the Holy Ghost. ("'It Becometh Every Man,'" *Ensign,* Oct. 1977, 3)

HOME TEACHING

The priesthood home teaching program can become a huge umbrella under which all the people of the Church may huddle for protection from the storms of adversity, sin, crime, delinquency, carelessness in activity, and immorality; but, of course, like an ordinary umbrella, if it is leaky and is not whole, stretched silk will be little protection. ("The Church Faces the Future in Missionary Work," Regional Representatives Conference, 25 Sept. 1967)

HONESTY

The theft of pennies or dollars or commodities may impoverish little the one from whom the goods are taken, but it is a shriveling, dwarfing process to the one who steals. ("'Whatsoever Things Are Honest,'" BYU, June 1958)

In every walk of life there are chances for the stories of dishonesty. Professional people are said to be charging prohibitive prices for service: "All that the law will allow." Colored water sold as a costly prescription, a few cents' worth of drugs for many dollars, poor material in the hidden places in building construction, improper billing, "cutting in" by clerks, so-called borrowing without consent by one entrusted with money. There is the workman who steals time, the employer who oppresses and takes advantage of his employees, the missionary who soldiers on the job, the speeder, the merchant selling inferior goods at marked-up prices, the constant close-out sales intended to misrepresent and deceive, the mark-up of prices in order to show remarkable sales values, the adjusted scales and measures, raising rents because of housing shortage not because of increased costs of maintenance or interest rates. ("'Whatsoever Things Are Honest,'" BYU, June 1958)

HONORING PARENTS AND GRANDPARENTS

My cousins, if we are sons and daughters of Heber C. Kimball in more than name, we shall do the works which he did, fight the battles he fought, espouse the cause to which he gave his life, and live the kind of righteous life to which he directed his great energies. Let us honor the memory of our illustrious grandfather by more than words; let us bring real honor to his name by a rededication of our lives and interests and possessions and talents to the service of our fellowmen and to our God with a devotion which tries to equal or surpass that of our forebear. That is what he would most want of us, as it is what we would most want of our children. (*Kimball Family News,* June 1979)

It is not enough to honor our parents in some narrow way. If we truly honor them, we will seek to emulate their best characteristics and to fulfill their highest aspirations for us. No gift purchased from a store can begin to match in value to parents some simple, sincere words of appreciation. Nothing we could give them would be more prized than righteous living for each youngster. Even where parents have not great strength of testimony, they will take pride in the strength and conviction of their children, if the relationship between them is a tolerant, loving, supporting one. (Independence Missouri Stake Center dedication, 3 Sept. 1978)

HUMAN RIGHTS

As members of Christ's true church we must stand firm today and always for human rights and the dignity of man, who is the literal offspring of God in the spirit. ("Fortify Your Homes Against Evil," *Ensign,* May 1979, 4)

HUMILITY

Humility is gracious, quiet, serene—not pompous, spectacular, nor histrionic. It is subdued, kindly, and understanding—not crude, blatant, loud, or ugly. Humility is not just a man or a woman but a perfect gentleman and a gentlelady. It never struts nor swaggers. Its faithful, quiet works will be the badge of its own accomplishments. It never sets itself in the center of the stage, leaving all others in supporting roles. Humility is never accusing nor contentious. It is not boastful. . . . When one becomes conscious of his great humility, he has already lost it. ("Humility," *Improvement Era,* Aug. 1963, 656)

HUNTING

I remember many times singing with a loud voice:

Don't kill the little birds, that sing on bush and tree,

All thro' the summer days, their sweetest melody.

Don't shoot the little birds! The earth is God's estate,

And he provideth food for small as well as great. (*Deseret Songs,* 1909, no. 163.)

I had a sling and I had a flipper. I made them myself, and they worked very well. It was my duty to walk the cows to pasture a mile away from home. There were large cottonwood trees lining the road, and I remember that it was quite a temptation to shoot the little birds "that sing on bush and tree," because I was a pretty good shot and I could hit a post at fifty yards' distance or I could hit the trunk of a tree. But I think perhaps because I sang nearly every Sunday, "Don't Kill the Little Birds," I was restrained. . . . I could see no great fun in having a beautiful little bird fall at my feet. ("Strengthening the Family—The Basic Unit of the Church," *Ensign,* May 1978, 45)

IDOLATRY

In all ages when men have fallen under the power of Satan and lost the faith, they have put in its place a hope in the "arm of flesh" and in "gods of silver, and gold, of brass, iron, wood, and stone, which see not, nor hear, nor know" (Daniel 5:23)—that is, in idols. This I find to be a dominant theme in the Old Testament. Whatever thing a man sets his heart and his trust in most is his god; and if his god doesn't also happen to be the true and living God of Israel, that man is laboring in idolatry. ("The False Gods We Worship," *Ensign,* June 1976, 3)

Modern idols or false gods can take such forms as clothes, homes, businesses, machines, automobiles, pleasure boats, and numerous other material deflectors from the path of godhood.

Intangible things make just as ready gods. Degrees and letters and titles can become idols.

. . . Still another image men worship is that of power and prestige. Many will trample underfoot the spiritual and often the ethical values in their climb to success. These gods of power, wealth, and influence are most demanding and are quite as real as the golden calves of the children of Israel in the wilderness. (*Miracle,* 40–42)

INTEGRITY

Are we trying to cover up the small pettiness and the small gratifications we secretly allow ourselves—rationalizing all the while that they are insignificant and inconsequential? Are there areas in our thoughts and actions and attitudes which we would like to hide from those we respect most? . . . "The rebellious shall be pierced with much sorrow; for their iniquities shall be spoken upon the housetops, and their secret acts shall be revealed." (D&C 1:3.) ("Honesty," LDS Businessmen's Association, San Francisco, 6 March 1967)

Integrity is one of the cornerstones of character. . . . Integrity is a state or quality of being complete, undivided, or unbroken. It is wholeness and unimpaired. It is purity and moral soundness. It is unadulterated genuineness and deep sincerity. It is courage, a human virtue of incalculable value. It is honesty, uprightness, and righteousness. Take these away and there is left but an empty shell.

Integrity in individuals and corporate bodies is not to ask, "What will others think of me and my practices?" but, "What do I think of myself, if I do this or fail to do that?" Is it proper? Is it right? Would the Master approve? . . .

Integrity in man should bring inner peace, sureness of purpose, and security in action. Lack of it brings the reverse: disunity, fear, sorrow, unsureness. ("Integrity in Insurance," Beneficial Life convention, Mexico City, 9 July 1970)

One might be smart and clever; one might be full of wit and humor; one might be dexterous in performance, but if he has not honor and integrity, he has little or nothing. ("Honor," Ricks College, 27 Sept. 1965)

JOURNALS

We urge our young people to begin today to write and keep records of all the important things in their own lives and also the lives of their antecedents in the event that their parents should fail to record all the important incidents in their own lives. . . . Your journal should contain your true self rather than a picture of you when you are "made up" for a public performance. There is a temptation to paint one's virtues in rich color and whitewash the vices, but there is also the opposite pitfall of accentuating the negative. . . .

What could you do better for your children and your children's children than to record the story of your life, your triumphs over adversity, your recovery after a fall, your progress when all seemed black, your rejoicing when you had finally achieved? . . .

Get a notebook, my young folks, a journal that will last through all time, and maybe the angels may quote from it for eternity. Begin today and write in it your goings and comings, your deepest thoughts, your achievements and your failures, your associations and your triumphs, your impressions and your testimonies. ("The Angels May Quote From It," *New Era,* Oct. 1975, 4)

KINDNESS TO ANIMALS

I had a father who was infuriated if he saw a man beating a balky horse, or kicking his dog, or starving his other animals. Wise Solomon said, "A righteous man regardeth the life of his beast." (Proverbs 12:10.) ("A Report and a Challenge," *Ensign,* Nov. 1976, 4)

KNOWLEDGE

I have learned that where there is a prayerful heart, a hungering after righteousness, a forsaking of sins, and obedience to the commandments of God, the Lord pours out more and more light until one finally has power to pierce the heavenly veil and to know more than man knows. Such a person has a priceless promise that one day he will see the Lord's face and know that He is (see D&C 93:1). ("Integrity: The Spirit of BYU," BYU, 4 Sept. 1979)

It is not so much what we know as what we do. The devil knew all, and yet lost all. Knowledge itself is not the end. Knowledge applied, of course, can bring us the testimony and the wisdom and can bring us to our goal—exaltation. ("The Ordinances of the Gospel," BYU, 18 June 1962)

LAMANITES

The Lamanites must rise again in dignity and strength to fully join their brethren and sisters of the household of God in carrying forth his work in preparation for that day when the Lord Jesus Christ will return to lead his people, when the Millennium will be ushered in, when the earth will be renewed and receive its paradisiacal glory and its lands be united and become one land. ("Our Paths Have Met Again," *Ensign,* Dec. 1975, 2)

Above all the problems the Indian has, his greatest one is the white man—the white man, who not only dispossessed him, but the white man who has never seemed to try to understand him—the white man who stands pharisaically above him—the white man who goes to the temple to pray and says, "Lord, I thank thee that I am not as other men are." The white man is his problem. ("The Lamanite," *Improvement Era,* April 1955, 226)

I plead with you to accept the Lamanite as your brother. I ask not for your tolerance—your cold, calculating tolerance; your haughty, contemptible tolerance; your scornful, arrogant tolerance; your pitying, coin-tossing tolerance. I ask you to give them what they want and need and deserve: opportunity and your fraternal brotherliness and your understanding; your warm and glowing fellowship; your unstinted and beautiful love; your enthusiastic and affectionate brotherhood. ("The Lamanite," *Improvement Era,* April 1955, 226)

If the Indians had all that was rightfully theirs they would not be where they are and we would not be where we are. Remember that.

We are here through the grace of God, and do not forget it. The Lord gave us to share an inheritance with the Indians in this glorious land which is choice above all other lands in all the world. But it is ours only on the condition, as I see it, that we do our part in seeing that these people come into the Church.

What the Lamanite needs is opportunity. The only difference between us and the Indian is opportunity. Give them an opportunity, sisters, so that they, too, can enjoy the blessings that you do.

("'Unwashen' Hands vs. Hearts," *Relief Society Magazine,* Dec. 1949, 804)

The chasm between what [the Indian] is and what he will be is opportunity. It is ours to give.

Basically the Indian is intelligent, affectionate, responsive, honest, stable, and is of believing blood. There is every reason to be assured that the red man will remain loyal and true to the gospel and the Church, once he is brought into the fold. ("'Who Is My Neighbor?'" *Improvement Era,* May 1949, 277)

LEADERS

I would not say that those leaders whom the Lord chooses are necessarily the most brilliant, nor the most highly trained, but they are the chosen, and when chosen of the Lord they are His recognized authority, and the people who stay close to them have safety. ("Be Valiant," *Improvement Era,* June 1951, 432)

Sometimes in the Church we have people who lose their faith because a bishop or a high councilor or a stake president goes astray. They fail to realize that all these people are also human, and while they have weaknesses they are striving to live better, but sometimes they succumb to the whirlpool of temptations about them. Sometimes in business transactions there are misunderstandings. . . . If we waited until we could find absolutely perfect people to man the organizations in the Church, we would never have an organization. The best that can be found under the circumstances are generally chosen to give leadership; and sometimes even those best ones fail. (Letter dated 22 Dec. 1955)

Goals are extremely important for every leader. It is well for him to set them himself for himself and induce his departments to set their own goals—goals that are realistic and can be reached but always greater than before; goals that are self-set and self-carried out. The leader should have a feedback system, a continuing inflow of knowledge so that he may know how well it works. ("The Image of a Stake," Regional Representatives Conference, 4 Oct. 1973)

The Lord made no mistake in His choice. The Lord knows that you and I are capable of doing the work to which He calls us. He makes no errors. But, if we fail to measure up in our responsibilities sometimes it looks like the Lord might have made a mistake. (Hamburg Stake Conference, 21 Jan. 1962)

Way down in southern Chile and in little cities up in northern Argentina, to see these people come long distances at great expense to be there to greet us, I felt tremendously humble, like bowing my head, as these people came in honor of one of our number here. Then I recognized again that I am but a symbol to them. They did not know me. They had never seen me. They came not to see me. They came to see the Apostle and their reverence and their interest was to the Church, to its leadership, to the program, and I was but a symbol, and it makes me humble indeed. (Meeting of the Council of the Twelve, 7 Dec. 1966)

LEADERSHIP

Do you think of leadership as telling others what to do, or as making all the decisions? Not so. Leadership is the ability to encourage the best efforts of others in working toward a desirable goal. Who has more significant opportunities to lead than a mother who guides her children toward perfection, or the wife who daily counsels with her husband that they may grow together? ("Relief Society: Its Promise and Potential," *Ensign,* March 1976, 2)

There is no place in this Church for masters or slaves. We are all equal, although we are deacons or Apostles. We have callings and responsibilities but we are all the sons of God and there is no reason for anyone to rise up in his majesty when he has a position of responsibility, and no place for any leader to lord it over others just because he has authority.

The Savior who was the head of the Church never ruled by force. (Lamanite Conference, Mesa, Arizona, 3 Nov. 1947)

Jesus demonstrated exemplary leadership. Jesus knew who He was and why He was here on this planet. That meant He could lead from strength rather than from uncertainty or weakness . . . , from a base of fixed principles or truths rather than making up the rules as He went along. Thus, His leadership style was not only correct, but also constant. Jesus said several times, "Come, follow me." His was a program of "do what I do," rather than "do what I say." The leaven of true leadership cannot lift others unless we are with and serve those to be led. . . .

Jesus was a listening leader. Because He loved others with a perfect love, He listened without being condescending. . . .

Because Jesus loved His followers, He was able to level with them, to be candid and forthright with them. He reproved Peter at times because He loved him, and Peter, being a great man, was able to grow from this reproof. . . . Jesus was not afraid to make demands of those He led. His leadership was not condescending or soft. He had the courage to call Peter and others to leave their fishing nets and to follow Him, not after the fishing season or after the next catch, but now! today! ("Jesus: The Perfect Leader," *Ensign,* Aug. 1979, 5)

LEGISLATION

We must work with all other good agencies to protect our youth, so far as we can by legislation, and laws and the enforcement thereof. But we must concede that our only totally effective weapon against the wiles of the devil is proper and preventive education and preventive training. The hands of the devil cannot be handcuffed nor the barred gates of his prison cell be locked but by the righteousness of his intended victims. ("What I Hope You Will Teach My Grandchildren," BYU, Seminary and Institute Teachers, 11 July 1966)

LOVE

The love of which the Lord speaks is not only physical attraction, but also faith, confidence, understanding, and partnership. It is devotion and companionship, parenthood, common ideals and standards. It is cleanliness of life and sacrifice and unselfishness. This kind of love never tires nor wanes. It lives on through sickness and sorrow, through prosperity and privation, through accomplishment and disappointment, through time and eternity. ("An Apostle Speaks About Marriage to John and Mary," *New Era,* June 1975, 2)

MARRIAGE

Husbands are commanded: "Love your wives, even as Christ also loved the church, and gave himself for it." (Ephesians 5:25.) Here is the answer: Christ loved the Church and its people so much that He voluntarily endured persecution for them, stoically withstood pain and physical abuse for them, and finally gave His precious life for them.

When the husband is ready to treat his household in that manner, not only the wife, but also all the family will respond to his leadership. ("Home Training—The Cure for Evil," *Improvement Era,* June 1965, 512)

In his wisdom and mercy, our Father made men and women dependent on each other for the full flowering of their potential. Because their natures are somewhat different, they can complement each other; because they are in many ways alike, they can understand each other. Let neither envy the other for their differences; let both discern what is superficial and what is beautifully basic in those differences, and act accordingly. ("Relief Society: Its Promise and Potential," *Ensign,* March 1976, 2)

In true marriage there must be a union of minds as well as of hearts. Emotions must not wholly determine decisions, but the mind and the heart, strengthened by fasting and prayer and serious consideration, will give one a maximum chance of marital happiness. ("The Matter of Marriage," University of Utah Institute of Religion, 22 Oct. 1976)

In family life, men must and should be considerate of their wives, not only in the bearing of children, but in caring for them through childhood. The mother's health must be conserved, and the husband's consideration for his wife is his first duty, and self-control a dominant factor in all their relationships. ("A Report and a Challenge," *Ensign,* Nov. 1976, 4)

Make yourself attractive as a marriage partner. . . . What are your eccentricities, if any? I think nearly all people have some. If so, then go to work. Classify them, weigh them, corral them, and eliminate one at a time until you are a very normal person. ("Small Acts of Service," *Ensign,* Dec. 1974, 2)

Many young people labor and live under false notions, feeling that a marriage contract, and especially if it is a temple marriage, solves all the problems; and many people further think that marriage is a sort of perpetual motion program. Once set in motion by a marriage ceremony, it will never run down. I want to tell you that there are no marriages that can ever be happy ones unless two people work at it. (Letter dated 5 Jan. 1960)

The ideal spouse is constant. While one is young and well and strong and beautiful or handsome and attractive, he or she can (for the moment) almost name the price and write the ticket; but the time comes when these temporary things have had their day; when wrinkles come and aching joints; when hair is thin and bodies bulge; when nerves are frayed and tempers are taut; when wealth is dissipated; when man needs something firm and solid to hold to. There comes a time when those who flattered us and those whose wit and charm deceived us may leave us to our fate. Those are times when we want friends, good friends, common friends, loved ones, tied with immortal bonds—people who will nurse our illnesses, tolerate our eccentricities, and love us with pure, undefiled affection. Then we need an unspoiled companion who will not count our wrinkles, remember our stupidities, nor remember our weaknesses; then is when we need a loving companion with whom we have suffered and wept and prayed and worshiped; one with whom we have suffered sorrow and disappointments, one who loves us for what we are or intend to be rather than what we appear to be in our gilded shell. (Letter dated 5 Jan. 1960)

To the large group of [unmarried] young women, we can only say, you are making a great contribution to the world as you serve your families and the Church and world. You must remember that the Lord loves you and the Church loves you. We have no control over the heartbeats or the affections of men, but pray that you may find total fulfillment. And in the meantime, we promise you that insofar as your eternity is concerned, that no soul will be deprived of rich, eternal blessings for anything which that person could not help, that eternity is a long time, and that the Lord never fails in His promises and that every righteous woman will receive eventually all to which she is entitled which she has not forfeited through any fault of her own. (Special Interest fireside, 29 Dec. 1974)

We need to make the marriage relationship sacred, to sacrifice and work to maintain the warmth and respect which we felt during courtship. God intended for marriage to be eternal, sealed by the power of the priesthood in the temples of the Lord. Daily acts of courtesy and kindness, conscientiously planned for, are part of what the Lord expects. (Independence Missouri Stake Center dedication, 3 Sept. 1978)

While marriage is difficult, and discordant and frustrated marriages are common, yet real, lasting happiness is possible, and marriage can be more an exultant ecstasy than the human mind can conceive. . . .

Two individuals approaching the marriage altar must realize that to attain the happy marriage which they hope for, they must know that marriage is not a legal cover-all; but it means sacrifice, sharing, and even a reduction of some personal liberties. It means long, hard economizing. It means children who bring with them financial burdens, service burdens, care and worry burdens; but it also means the deepest and sweetest emotions of all. ("Marriage and Divorce," BYU, 7 Sept. 1976)

Young women should plan and prepare for marriage and the bearing and rearing of children. It is your divine right and the avenue to the greatest and most supreme happiness. You should also make choices looking forward to productive use of your time once the children are grown and gone from under your wing. You should seek for ways to bless the lives of all with whom you associate. You should know the truth of all things. You should be prepared to help build the kingdom of God. . . .

There is a great and grand principle involved here. Just as those who do not hear the gospel in this life, but who would have received it with all their hearts had they heard it, will be given the fulness of the gospel blessings in the next world—so, too, the women of the Church who do not in this life have the privileges and blessings of a temple marriage, through no fault of their own, who would have responded if they had an appropriate opportunity—will receive all those blessings in the world to come. ("Privileges and Responsibilities of Sisters," *Ensign,* Nov. 1978, 102)

MARTYRDOM

Martyrs do not die. They live on and on. When the Savior said, "It is finished," He referred to His mortal experience, for His crucifixion marked but a milepost in His ever-expanding power. Hundreds of millions have been influenced for good by this perfect life and martyr's death. He had said Himself: "And whoso layeth down his life in my cause, for my name's sake, shall find it again." (D&C 98:13.) His work continues to spread to this day. ("The Pattern of Martyrdom," *Improvement Era,* May 1946, 286)

Men do not give their lives to perpetuate falsehoods. Martyrdom dissipates all question as to the sincerity of the martyr. "Personalities" do not survive the ages. They rise like a shooting star, shine brilliantly for a moment, and disappear from view, but a martyr for a living cause, like the sun, shines on forever. ("The Pattern of Martyrdom," *Improvement Era,* May 1946, 286)

MILLENNIUM

When Satan is bound in a single home—when Satan is bound in a single life—the Millennium has already begun in that home, in that life. ("Follow Leaders," University of Utah Institute of Religion, 14 April 1968)

MIRACLES

Many would like to have the miracle to build their faith, but it is the result rather than the cause of faith. Rationalization can soon void and nullify a miracle if it has not a foundation of faith to precede it. Miracles of today can be argued and rationalized away at times as they could in days of old. ("The Priesthood," Salt Lake City Monument Park Stake Conference, 12 Sept. 1976)

MISSIONARY WORK

Lose yourself in this work, and all who lose themselves will find themselves. Forget the things of pleasure and self and, consistent with good health, consecrate yourself and energies to the work, and you will find the magnificent obsession that what you want most to do is to touch souls. (Lamanite Conference, Mesa, Arizona, 4 Nov. 1947)

But I can see no good reason why the Lord would open doors that we are not prepared to enter. Why should He break down the Iron Curtain or the Bamboo Curtain or any other curtain if we are still unprepared to enter? ("'The Uttermost Parts of the Earth,'" *Ensign,* July 1979, 2)

Don't let any boy grow to maturity without having been interviewed for a mission. Now, some of them may not be worthy. Some of them may have been immoral. Some of them may not care, and maybe they will not repent. But most of your boys, if you start very young with them when they are just little boys, will stay clean. And they'll save their money. They'll be expecting a mission, they'll go on missions, and they'll bring into this Church millions of people through the years.

And they'll do something else. While they are in the mission field they'll grow and develop like a blossoming plant. You've seen it and we've seen it. (Sao Paulo Area Conference, 1 March 1975)

Humility is essential in missionary work. To convince people of the divinity of the work one must of necessity be humble. To be arrogant or "cocky" is to threaten to drive away the Holy Ghost, who alone can convince and bring testimonies. (Message for Houston Texas Stake missionaries, Sept. 1958)

Let us make that the rule—that every boy ought to go on a mission. There may be some who can't, but they *ought* to go on a mission. Every boy, and many girls, and many couples. We could use hundreds of couples, older people like some of you folks, whose families are reared, who have retired in their business, who are able to go and spend their own money to teach the gospel. We could use hundreds of couples. You just go and talk to your bishop—that is all you need to do. Tell him, "We are ready to go, if you can use us." I think you will probably get a call. (Fair Oaks California Stake Center dedication, 9 Oct. 1976)

Now is the moment in the timetable of the Lord to carry the gospel farther than it has ever been carried before—farther geographically, and farther in density of coverage. Many a person in this world is crying, knowingly and unknowingly, "Come over . . . and help us." He might be your neighbor. She might be your friend. He might be a relative. She might be someone you met only yesterday. But we have what they need. Let us take new courage from our studies and pray, as did Peter, "And now, Lord, . . . grant unto thy servants, that with all boldness they may speak thy word." (Acts 4:29.) ("Always a Convert Church," *Ensign,* Sept. 1975, 2)

One should study, ponder, learn scriptures, and build his testimony so that he may be prepared to teach and train. The Lord has said, "If ye are prepared ye shall not fear" (D&C 38:30), and it is our hope that from infancy through all the years of maturing, the lessons taught in the auxiliaries, in the seminaries and institutes, in the home evenings, in the sacrament meetings, and elsewhere may bring every youth to a preparation that will eliminate fear. Every person approaching a mission should be schooled, trained, and indoctrinated for immediate and proper participation in proselyting. Gospel doctrine or organization illiteracy should never be found among our youth. Proper scriptures can be learned well and permanently by children; doctrines can be taught and absorbed by youth. ("Advice to a Young Man: Now Is the Time to Prepare," *New Era,* June 1973, 8)

We could make a different mistake by too-brazen trumpeting of our motives for acting as we do, but most of us err on the other side. We fail to find some quiet way to let our colleagues at work and in social organizations and in our neighborhood know that we are first of all, and always, followers of Jesus Christ. (Independence Missouri Stake Center dedication, 3 Sept. 1978)

When I ask for more missionaries, I am not asking for more testimony-barren or unworthy missionaries. I am asking that we start earlier and train our missionaries better in every branch and every ward in the world. That is another challenge—that the young people will understand that it is a great privilege to go on a mission and that they must be physically well, mentally well, spiritually well, and that "the Lord cannot look upon sin with the least degree of allowance." (D&C 1:31.)

I am asking for missionaries who have been carefully indoctrinated and trained through the family and the organizations of the Church, and who come to the mission with a great desire. I am asking for better interviews, more searching interviews, more sympathetic and understanding interviews, but especially that we train prospective missionaries much better, much earlier, much longer, so that each anticipates his mission with great joy. ("'When the World Will Be Converted,'" *Ensign,* Oct. 1974, 2)

With such a noble work one should not find it too difficult to develop enthusiasm. Enthusiasm is real interest plus dedicated energy, and this combination provides the most dynamic of all human qualities. But anyone who does not have it naturally can cultivate it by applying autosuggestion. Merely deciding that a job is going to be interesting helps to make it so. ("Integrity in Insurance," Beneficial Life convention, Mexico City, 9 July 1970)

You are not [on a mission] for your own comforts and conveniences and desires. You did not go to see the world or get experiences. You went to forget

yourself into immortality, and while in total forget-
fulness of yourself, you would bring many to total
conversion to the truth. . . . The mere call to a mission does not transform a boy, but it does provide
an unusual opportunity for him to improve himself and develop his powers and spirit. . . . My dear
boy, we all have our crosses. If we can get rid of
them we do, but if we can't we carry them and go
about our life's work. . . . Maybe you need to sit
down and "count your blessings." . . . I hope you
will take proper steps to get to the bottom of your
trouble and cure it if possible; then move forward
to forget yourself and remember the millions of
good people about you who are perishing for want
of what you can take to them. . . . It is on the second mile where the honest in heart are often
found. It is in the extra dozen homes which are
contacted after the "time to quit" has come that the
new leader converts generally live. (Letter dated 14
Jan. 1958)

Your faith and knowledge of truth are the result
of missionary work of days gone by, which you
can repay only by giving to others the same
opportunities. Hence it is well for every worthy
and prepared young man, as he grows up, to
desire mightily to fill a mission. Of course, there
is no compulsion. Each person makes up his
mind on this matter as he does in receiving the

priesthood, paying his tithes, marrying in the temple, serving in the Church. He ought to do all these things, but has his free agency. ("Advice to a Young Man: Now Is the Time to Prepare," *New Era,* June 1973, 8)

I am not convinced that mission presidents should ever set goals for missionaries. They may set goals for their mission if they like, and for themselves, but let the missionaries set goals for themselves and then the president will praise and give them adulation for succeeding in the goals which they set. (Seminar for New Mission Presidents, 20 June 1975)

MUSIC

Musical sounds can be put together in such a way that they can express feelings—from the most profoundly exalted to the most abjectly vulgar. Or rather, these musical sounds induce in the listener feelings which he responds to, and the response he makes to these sounds has been called a "gesture of the spirit." Thus, music can act upon our senses to produce or induce feelings of reverence, humility, fervor, assurance, or other feelings attuned to the spirit of worship. ("How to Use Music More Effectively," 22 Jan. 1968)

MYSTERIES

We must admit that there are many mysteries of the kingdom. I am sure that the Lord will reveal them as fast as we are ready for them. We have enough to save and exalt us now. A small percentage of the people are living up to those teachings. The Brethren are united on all policies and programs, but when they go beyond the revealed word and they enter the field of conjecture, there will come differences of opinion. (Letter dated 31 May 1948)

ORDINANCES

Clearly, attaining eternal life is not a matter of goodness only. That is one of the two important elements, but one must practice righteousness and receive the ordinances. People who do not bring their lives into harmony with God's laws and who do not receive the necessary ordinances either in this life or (if that is impossible) in the next, have thus deprived themselves, and will remain separate and single in the eternities. There they will have no spouses, no children. (*Miracle,* 245)

Now the ordinances of the gospel are vital. Someday we must know all about them. We cannot imagine becoming gods ourselves until we know all things. A little child doesn't need to know all about the blessing. He may not fully comprehend all of the blessings of baptism when he is eight. One may not fully understand the full significance of the sacrament. And in like manner, one doesn't need to know all about electricity to enjoy its benefits. We encourage the gaining of knowledge, but keep in mind that it is the doing of the commandments that is the important thing. ("The Ordinances of the Gospel," BYU, 18 June 1962)

All these ordinances are futile unless with them there is a great righteousness. . . . So we go out into every field to perfect our lives. It is not enough to pay tithing and live the Word of Wisdom. We must be chaste in mind and in body. We must be neighborly, kind, and clean of heart. Sometimes people feel if they have complied with the more mechanical things that they are in line. And yet perhaps their hearts are not always pure. (Swiss Temple dedication, 15 Sept. 1955)

PARENTS

On a cold winter day most children set out for school warmly clothed. The soles of their shoes are thick, and they wear boots over them. They wear heavy coats, with scarves around their necks and mittens on their hands—all to protect them from the inclemency of the weather. But are these same children protected against the mistaken ideologies and ideas of other youth and the temptations of the day? ("'Train Up a Child,'" *Ensign,* April 1978, 2)

PASSIVITY

[There] are Church members who are steeped in lethargy. They neither drink nor commit sexual sins. They do not gamble nor rob nor kill. They are good citizens and splendid neighbors, but spiritually speaking they seem to be in a long, deep sleep. They are doing nothing seriously wrong except in their failures to do the right things to earn their exaltation. To such people as this, the words of Lehi might well apply: "O that ye would awake; awake from a deep sleep, yea, even from the sleep of hell, and shake off the awful chains by which ye are bound, which are the chains which bind the children of men, that they are carried away captive down to the eternal gulf of misery and woe." (2 Nephi 1:13.) (*Miracle,* 211–12)

I guess we as humans are prone to forget. It is easy to forget. Our sorrows, our joys, our concerns, our great problems seem to wane to some extent as time goes on, and there are many lessons that we learn which have a tendency to slip from us. The Nephites forgot. They forgot the days when they felt good. (Council of the Twelve meeting, 8 March 1967)

People tend often to measure their righteousness by the absence of wrong acts in their lives, as if passivity were the end of being. But God has created "things to act and things to be acted upon" (2 Nephi 2:14), and man is in the former category. He does not fill the measure of his creation unless he acts, and that in righteousness. "Therefore to him that knoweth to do good, and doeth it not," warns James, "to him it is sin." (James 4:17.)

To be passive is deadening; to stop doing is to die. Here then is a close parallel with physical life. If one fails to eat and drink, his body becomes emaciated and dies. Likewise, if he fails to nourish his spirit and mind, his spirit shrivels and his mind darkens. (*Miracle,* 91–93)

PATRIARCHAL BLESSING

Patriarchal blessings are revelations to the recipients—a white line down the middle of the road to protect, inspire, and motivate toward activity and righteousness.

An inspired patriarchal blessing could light the way and lead the recipient on a path to fulfillment. It could lead him to become a new man and to have in his body a new heart. (Sermon to patriarchs of the Church, 3 Oct. 1969)

The blessings which the patriarch gives are conditional. They are promised, as are most other blessings that the Lord has promised to people, contingent upon their worthiness and fulfilling the obligations. There is no guarantee that the blessings will be fulfilled unless the individual subscribes to the program, but I bear my testimony to you that none of the blessings he pronounces will fail if the participant of the blessing fully subscribes. (Seoul Area Conference, 17 Aug. 1975)

PEACE

Peace is the fruit of righteousness. It cannot be bought with money, and cannot be traded nor bartered. It must be earned. The wealthy often spend much of their gains in a bid for peace, only to find that it is not for sale. But the poorest as well as the richest may have it in abundance if the total price is paid. Those who abide the laws and live the Christlike life may have peace and other kindred blessings, principal among which are exaltation and eternal life. They include also blessings for this life. (*Miracle,* 363–64)

Tranquility of soul, joy, and peace are the fruits of right living. . . . Peace is when you can turn a corner without apprehension and look in the eye those you meet; it is the supremacy over fear, not fearlessness, but the courage to go forward in spite of fear; it is the hearing of the telephone bell without a start; the opening of your door to the police without a quiver; the receiving of a telegram without a tremble.

Peace is when the fracture is knit; when the chasm is bridged; when the villagers come home at night from their fields knowing where they will sleep; when the grain is stored in the barn; the folded linen is piled in the drawer and the fruit is canned and stored in the cupboard. ("The Peace Which Passeth Understanding," BYU, 4 June 1944)

Christ was not a political victor. The harbinger of peace was not accepted nor received by His people, for the brand of peace He offered was not the kind they had been expecting. Long centuries they had looked for a redeemer, but their interpretations of the numerous prophecies left them expecting a warrior to lead them victoriously against their political enemies and free them from Roman bondage. Wishful thinking and ambitious hopes had led them to look for a redeemer who would reign with the sword, as a political king, and put under his feet all kingdoms and dominions. . . .

Yet such a peace was never contemplated by the Lord, nor was such an one ever prophesied. But He did bring emancipation to a benighted world, to a people bound in the chains of superstition, lip service, and spiritual bondage. He came and organized His church, set up an eternal program, loosed the bands of death through His own death and resurrection, and outlined and lived before us a perfect plan by which all men might live eternally in joy and peace. ("The Peace Which Passeth Understanding," BYU, 4 June 1944)

PERFECTION

I have little patience with persons who say, "Oh, nobody is perfect," the implication being: "so why try?" Of course no one is wholly perfect, but we find some who are a long way up the ladder. (BYU Student Leadership Conference, Sun Valley, Idaho, Sept. 1958)

Perfection is not a one-time decision to be made, but a process to be pursued, slowly and laboriously through a lifetime. We build from simple building blocks, adding refinements as the building rises towards the heavens. . . . Jesus taught His followers the sanctity of the Ten Commandments, but pointed out repeatedly that there was more to do yet. . . . As the Lord asked him [the rich young man] to take on a more difficult task after he had mastered the lesser ones, so as we gain strength from keeping the simpler commandments, the Lord will ask us to undertake greater tasks with this new strength. (Independence Missouri Stake Center dedication, 3 Sept. 1978)

As we have stated before, the way to perfection seems to be a changing of one's life—to substitute the good for the evil in every case. Changes can come best if we take one item at a time. For instance, it is not difficult to be perfect in tithe paying, for if one pays one-tenth of his income annually, he is perfect in that respect. It is not difficult to become perfect in avoiding a swearing habit, for if one locks his mouth against all words of cursing, he is en route to perfection in that matter. ("Be Ye Therefore Perfect," BYU, 17 Sept. 1974)

This life, this narrow sphere we call mortality, does not, within the short space of time we are allowed here, give to all of us perfect justice, perfect health, or perfect opportunities. Perfect justice, however, will come eventually through a divine plan, as will the perfection of all other conditions and blessings—to those who have lived to merit them. ("The Abundant Life," *Ensign,* July 1978, 3)

The cultivation of Christlike qualities is a demanding and relentless task—it is not for the seasonal worker or for those who will not stretch themselves, again and again. ("Privileges and Responsibilities of Sisters," *Ensign,* Nov. 1978, 102)

PERSECUTION

Do not be puzzled if sometimes there are those in the world who mock how you live and what you believe, saying it is all false, but who, deep inside themselves, are really afraid that what you believe is really true. ("The Savior: The Center of Our Lives," *New Era,* April 1980, 33)

PIONEERS

Let us not lose the "Winter Quarters" habit of starting crops to be harvested by those who follow. Let us be pioneers (for our people yet to be born) by planting the wheat of our witness, that those who follow us may eat of the bread of belief in time of famine elsewhere in the world! ("Boys Need Heroes Close By," *Ensign,* May 1976, 45)

POLITICS

Please avoid, even by implication, involving the Church in political issues. It is so easy, if we are not careful, to project our personal preferences as the position of the Church on an issue. ("Boys Need Heroes Close By," *Ensign,* May 1976, 45)

PORNOGRAPHY

Be concerned about the types of programs your family is watching on television or hearing on radio. There is so much today that is unsavory and degrading, so much that gives the impression that the old sins of Sodom and Gomorrah are the "in thing" to do today. ("Strengthening the Family—The Basic Unit of the Church," *Ensign,* May 1978, 45)

POTENTIAL OF MAN

Each of us is a son or daughter of God, and has a responsibility to measure up, finally returning to Him with a perfected Christlike life of self-mastery. (*Youth,* 91)

In each of us is the potentiality to become a god— pure, holy, influential, true, and independent of all these earth forces. We learn from the scriptures that each of us has an eternal existence, that we were in the beginning with God. And understanding this gives to us a unique sense of man's dignity. (Buenos Aires Area Conference, 29 Oct. 1978)

Man can transform himself and he must. Man has in himself the seeds of godhood, which can germinate and grow and develop. As the acorn becomes the oak, the mortal man becomes a god. It is within his power to lift himself by his very bootstraps from the plane on which he finds himself to the plane on which he should be. It may be a long, hard lift with many obstacles, but it is a real possibility. ("Be Ye Therefore Perfect," BYU, 17 Sept. 1974)

May I assure you of the everlasting significance of your personal life. And even though at times the range of your life may seem to be very small, there can be greatness in the quality of your life. . . .

There must be an assembling in you of those basic qualities of goodness which will permit the Lord to do His own sculpting on your soul. Use, therefore, the talents that you have. Use the opportunities for service around you. Use the chances for learning that are yours, sifting as always the wheat from the chaff. Learn to be effective first in the small human universe that is your own family if you would prepare yourselves to be effective in contributing to the larger human family. ("The Savior: The Center of Our Lives," *New Era,* April 1980, 33)

The gospel is a program, a way of life, the plan of personal salvation, and is based on personal responsibility. It is developed for man, the offspring of God. Man is a god in embryo and has in him the seeds of godhood, and he can, if he will, rise to great heights. He can lift himself by his own bootstraps as no other creature can do. He was created not to fail and degenerate but to rise to perfection like his Lord Jesus Christ. (BYU, 16 July 1964)

PRAYER

A mother may pray with her children and call down the Lord's blessings upon them. She does not act by virtue of priesthood conferred upon her, but by virtue of her God-given responsibility to govern her household in righteousness. ("Ocean Currents and Family Influences," *Ensign,* Nov. 1974, 110)

Do you want to do what is best for you in the long run or what seems more desirable for the moment? Have you prayed? How much have you prayed? How did you pray? Have you prayed as did the Savior of the world in Gethsemane, or did you ask for what you want regardless of its being proper? Do you say in your prayers: "Thy will be done"? Did you say, "Heavenly Father, if you will inspire and impress me with the right, I will do that right"? Or, did you pray, "Give me what I want"? (Letter, undated)

"If any man will do his will, he shall know of the doctrine." (John 7:17.) The turning on of the radio can bring to us at once music, sermon, news in our physical world. A humble prayer on bended knees, followed by the other works, is the invisible switch to tune us with the infinite and bring to us programs of knowledge, inspiration, and faith. ("Spiritual Vision," BYU, 19 March 1946)

One cannot receive eternal life without becoming a "doer of the word" (see James 1:22) and being valiant in obedience to the Lord's commandments. And one cannot become a "doer of the word" without first becoming a "hearer." And to become a "hearer" is not simply to stand idly by and wait for chance bits of information; it is to seek out and study and pray and comprehend. ("How Rare a Possession—The Scriptures!" *Ensign,* Sept. 1976, 2)

I said, "How often do you pray?" "Well, not so very often." "Why don't you pray?" "I am not sure anymore." "Why aren't you sure anymore? Is it because you have cut all the communication lines?" You have lost His address. You do not have His telephone number even. How do you expect to know whether He is living or dead? If you went for two years without ever hearing from your parents and they were in the opposite end of the world, how would you know if they were alive or dead? How do you know if God is dead or alive if you have lost communication? Now, you get on your knees, my boy. If you want to be happy, get on your knees and crawl on your knees to the city of happiness. Only there is peace. (Missionary Conference, Cordoba, Argentina, 17 Nov. 1966)

If one rises from his knees having merely said words, he should fall back on his knees and remain there until he has established communication with the Lord, who is very anxious to bless, but having given man his free agency, will not force Himself upon that man. (Letter dated 4 May 1970)

In the family prayer there is even more than the supplication and prayer of gratitude. It is a forward step toward family unity and family solidarity. It builds family consciousness and establishes a spirit of family interdependence. Here is a moment of the rushed day with blatant radios hushed, lights low, and all minds and hearts turned to each other and to the infinite; a moment when the world is shut out and heaven enclosed within. ("Family Prayer," *Children's Friend,* Jan. 1946, 30)

Let me tell you about the little Indian child who came into the home of a white family in the West here for the year to go to school. The little child came in very timidly, and the day passed on, and finally it came time for the evening meal. When they came to the table, the foster father and mother took hold of their chairs, as to pull them out and sit in them, and then they happened to notice that down at her chair was a little Indian girl kneeling. They must have made a very quick decision. It must have been a rather difficult one to make, a decision that meant that they either had to explain to this little girl that they did not have family prayers, or they had to break a custom of their lifetime, and so two people who had never before been on their knees knelt down with the little Indian girl in the first family prayer of their married life. ("'That Ye May Bring Souls Unto Me,'" Primary Conference, 1 April 1955)

No mother would carelessly send her little children forth to school on a wintry morning without warm clothes to protect against the snow and rain and cold. But there are numerous fathers and mothers who send their children to school without the protective covering available to them through prayer—a protection against exposure to unknown hazards, evil people, and base temptations. (*Faith,* 207)

Prayer is the passport to spiritual power. ("The Family Influence," *Ensign,* July 1973, 15)

Remember that our prayers are often as inconsistent and inappropriate to our Father in Heaven as are the demands of our little children upon us. What earthly parent would give to a little one a bottle of poison with which to play, even though the child might ask for it and demand it and cry for it? Or who of you would turn a four- or six-year-old child loose with a powerful automobile, in spite of the fact that he insisted and pleaded for it? And yet we sometimes ask for just such impossible things, just such dangerous things, and the Lord in His mercy withholds them. Let us pray with the attitude always of the crucified One, "Nevertheless not my will, but thine, be done." (Luke 22:42.) ("Prayer," address over KGLU Radio, Safford, Arizona, 11 Sept. 1938)

Some things are best prayed over only in private, where time and confidentiality are not considerations. If in these special moments of prayer we hold back from the Lord, it may mean that some blessings may be withheld from us. After all, we pray as petitioners before an all-wise Heavenly Father, so why should we ever think to hold back feelings or thoughts which bear upon our needs and our blessings? We hope that our people will have very bounteous prayers.

It would not hurt us, either, if we paused at the end of our prayers to do some intense listening—even for a moment or two—always praying, as the Savior did, "not my will, but thine, be done." (Luke 22:42.) ("We Need a Listening Ear," *Ensign,* Nov. 1979, 4)

The children will learn to honor and revere the Lord's anointed leaders as they are taught to pray for their local and general authorities; they will love the Lord as they pray for His work; they will love their fellowmen as they pray for the sick, the mourners, the distressed. They will anticipate with gladness their own missions as they pray for the missionaries out preaching the gospel. ("Family Prayer," *Children's Friend,* Jan. 1946, 30)

The Lord has not promised us freedom from adversity and affliction. Instead, He has given us the avenue of communication known as prayer, whereby we might humble ourselves and seek His help and divine guidance. ("Remember the Mission of the Church," *Ensign,* May 1982, 4)

The Lord stands knocking. He never retreats. But He will never force Himself upon us. If our distance from Him increases, it is we who have moved and not the Lord. (*Faith,* 208)

We pray for enlightenment, then go to with all our might and our books and our thoughts and righteousness to get the inspiration. We ask for judgment, then use all our powers to act wisely and develop wisdom. We pray for success in our work and then study hard and strive with all our might to help answer our prayers. When we pray for health we must live the laws of health and do all in our power to keep our bodies well and vigorous. We pray for protection and then take reasonable precaution to avoid danger. There must be works with faith. How foolish it would be to ask the Lord to give us knowledge, but how wise to ask the Lord's help to acquire knowledge, to study constructively, to think clearly, and to retain things that we have learned. How stupid to ask the Lord to protect us if we unnecessarily drive at excessive speeds, or if we eat or drink destructive elements or try foolhardy stunts. (*Faith,* 205)

We pray for our enemies. This will soften our hearts, and perhaps theirs, and we may better seek good in them. And this prayer should not be confined to national enemies but should extend to neighbors, members of the family, and all with whom we have differences. (*Faith,* 203)

In many countries, the homes are barren and the cupboards bare—no books, no radios, no pictures, no furniture, no fire—while we are housed adequately, clothed warmly, fed extravagantly. Did we show our thanks by the proper devotion on our knees last night and this morning and tomorrow morning? ("The Most Perfect Personage Was the Most Perfect Teacher," Seminary and Institute Teachers Conference, 12 Sept. 1975)

PRIESTHOOD

One breaks the priesthood covenant by transgressing commandments—but also by leaving undone his duties. Accordingly, to break this covenant one needs only to do nothing. (*Miracle,* 96)

The priesthood is the power and authority of God delegated to man on earth to act in all things pertaining to the salvation of men. It is the means whereby the Lord acts through men to save souls. Without this priesthood power, men are lost. Only through this power does man "hold the keys of all the spiritual blessings of the church," enabling him to receive "the mysteries of the kingdom of heaven, to have the heavens opened" unto him (see D&C 107:18–19), enabling him to enter the new and everlasting covenant of marriage and to have his wife and children bound to him in an everlasting tie, enabling him to become a patriarch to his posterity forever, and enabling him to receive a fullness of the blessings of the Lord. ("The Example of Abraham," *Ensign,* June 1975, 3)

We had the glorious experience of having the Lord indicate clearly that the time had come when all worthy men and women everywhere can be fellow heirs and partakers of the full blessings of the gospel. I want you to know, as a special witness of the Savior, how close I have felt to Him and to our Heavenly Father as I have made numerous visits to the upper rooms in the temple, going on some days several times by myself. The Lord made it very clear to me what was to be done. We do not expect the people of the world to understand such things, for they will always be quick to assign their own reasons or to discount the divine process of revelation. ("The Savior: The Center of Our Lives," *New Era,* April 1980, 33)

PROCRASTINATION

One of the most serious human defects in all ages is procrastination, an unwillingness to accept personal responsibilities *now*. Men came to earth consciously to obtain their schooling, their training and development, and to perfect themselves, but many have allowed themselves to be diverted and have become merely "hewers of wood and drawers of water," addicts to mental and spiritual indolence and to the pursuit of worldly pleasure.

There are even many members of the Church who are lax and careless and who continually procrastinate. They live the gospel casually but not devoutly. They have complied with some requirements but are not valiant. They do no major crime but merely fail to do the things required—things like paying tithing, living the Word of Wisdom, having family prayers, fasting, attending meetings, serving. (*Miracle,* 8)

RACIAL PREJUDICE

Take this message back to your people in the stakes, that they leave off their racial prejudice. Racial prejudice is of the devil. Racial prejudice is of ignorance. There is no place for it in the gospel

of Jesus Christ. ("'Unwashen' Hands vs. Hearts,"
Relief Society Magazine, Dec. 1949, 804)

REPENTANCE

No one can ever be forgiven of any transgression
until there is repentance, and one has not repented
until he has bared his soul and admitted his inten-
tions and weaknesses without excuses, or rationalizations. When one admits that his sin is as big as it
really is, then he is ready to begin his repentance.
("Love vs. Lust," *Instructor,* April 1967, 138)

If we are humble and desirous of living the gospel
we will come to think of repentance as applying
to everything we do in life, whether it be spiritual
or temporal in nature. Repentance is for every
soul who has not yet reached perfection. (*Miracle,*
32–33)

In abandoning sin one cannot merely wish for
better conditions. He must make them. He may
need to come to hate the spotted garments and
loathe the sin. He must be certain not only that
he has abandoned the sin but that he has changed
the situations surrounding the sin. He should
avoid the places and conditions and cirsum-
stances where the sin occurred, for these could

most readily breed it again. He must abandon the people with whom the sin was committed. He may not hate the persons involved but he must avoid them and everything associated with the sin. . . . The things which engaged him and caught his fancy and occupied his thoughts are gone, and better substitutions have not yet filled the void. This is Satan's opportunity. . . . Victory in the fight to abandon sin depends on constant vigilance. . . . Satan will not readily let go. Rather, he will probably send a host of new temptations to weaken the resolve of the repentant one. (*Miracle,* 171–72, 86)

Repentance is a kind and merciful law. It is so far-reaching and all-inclusive. It has many elements and includes a sorrow for sin, a confession of sin, an abandonment of sin, a restitution for sin, and then the living of the commandments of the Lord, and this includes the forgiveness of others, even the forgiving of those who sin against us. ("'Except Ye Repent . . . ,'" *Improvement Era,* Nov. 1949, 712)

I am grateful for the Lord's longsuffering. He seems to get so little in return for His investment in us. However, the principle of repentance—of rising again whenever we fall, brushing ourselves off, and setting off again on that upward trail—is the basis for our hope. It is through repentance that the Lord Jesus Christ can work His healing miracle, infusing us with strength when we are weak, health when we are sick, hope when we are downhearted, love when we feel empty, and understanding when we search for truth. ("Integrity: The Spirit of BYU," BYU, 4 Sept. 1979)

Repentance must be as universal as is sin. ("'Except Ye Repent . . . ,'" *Improvement Era,* Nov. 1949, 712)

True repentance incorporates within it a washing, a purging, a changing of attitudes, a reappraising, a strengthening toward self-mastery. It is not a simple matter for one to transform his life overnight, nor to change attitudes in a moment, nor to rid himself in a hurry of unworthy companions. ("What Is True Repentance?" *Ensign,* May 1974, 4)

Very frequently people think they have repented and are worthy of forgiveness when all they have done is to express sorrow or regret at the unfortunate happening, but their repentance is barely started. Until they have begun to make changes in their lives, transformation in their habits, and to add new thoughts to their minds, to be sorry is only a bare beginning. ("What Is True Repentance?" *Ensign,* May 1974, 4)

While repentance is possible at any stage in the process of sin it is certainly easier in the early stages. Sinful habits may be compared to a river which flows slowly and placidly at first, then gains speed as it nears the falls over the precipice. Where it is slow and quiet, one can cross it in a rowboat with relative ease. As the stream flows faster it becomes more difficult to cross, but this is still possible. As the water nears the falls, it becomes almost a superhuman effort to row across without being swept mercilessly over the falls. (*Miracle*, 168)

You are "kicking against the pricks," my friend. You are swimming alone in a turbulent sea when you could have a raft or a rescue boat. You have done nothing yet of which you could not be forgiven, for the Lord is merciful and compassionate, but the day can come when all rescue boats will sail on to shore without you and it can be a wide, desolate sea. I am praying that I might say the right thing that would stir you to save yourself. (Letter, undated)

RESTITUTION

"A broken heart and a contrite spirit" will usually find ways to restore to some extent. The true spirit of repentance demands that he who injures shall do everything in his power to right the wrong. (*Miracle,* 195)

Repentance requires restitution where possible. The sinner should make restitution. It is obvious that the murderer cannot give back a life he has taken; the libertine cannot restore the virtue he has violated; the gossip may be unable to nullify and overcome the evils done by a loose tongue; but, so far as is possible, one must restore and make good the damage done. ("'Except Ye Repent . . . ,'" *Improvement Era,* Nov. 1949, 712)

RESTORATION

In our own dispensation . . . apostasy had covered the earth and gross darkness the people, and the minds of men were clouded and light had been obscured in darkness. The time had come. Religious liberty would protect the seed until it could germinate and grow. And the individual was prepared in the person of a youth, clean and open-minded, who had such implicit faith in the response of God that the heavens could not remain as iron and the earth as brass as they had been for many centuries. ("'For They Shall See God,'" *Improvement Era,* June 1964, 496)

Another day dawned, another soul with passionate yearning prayed for divine guidance. A spot of hidden solitude was found, knees were bended, hearts were humbled, pleadings were voiced, and a light brighter than the noonday sun illuminated the world—the curtain never to be closed again, the gate never again to be slammed, this light never again to be extinguished. A young lad of incomparable faith broke the spell, shattered the "heavens of iron" and reestablished communication. Heaven kissed the earth, light dissipated the darkness, and God again spake to man revealing "his secret unto his servants the prophets." (Amos 3:7.) A new prophet was in the land, and through him God set up his kingdom—a kingdom never to be destroyed nor left to another people—a kingdom that will stand forever. ("'To His Servants the Prophets,'" *Instructor,* Aug. 1960, 256)

He [Luther] did not expect to organize a new church. He just wanted to cleanse the old church, of which he was a priest. Now, we believe Luther was a great man. He was courageous. Yet, he did not claim revelation, as far as I have found; but he did a great service to mankind. He turned the key in the lock that opened the door of mental serfdom. For hundreds of years before Luther, there had been mental slavery. People did not read their Bibles, they listened only to the priest. They were in spiritual bondage. But beginning with this break of Martin Luther from the church of which he had been a member, freedom of thought and freedom of religion began to be a nearer reality. We know that Luther came as a servant of the Lord to open the way, just like Columbus discovered America in the part of the great program of our Heavenly Father, and just like the Puritans and Pilgrims who found their way to the new world. ("Revelation," article for the Swedish Mission, June 1955)

RESURRECTION

Being mortal and divine, and having suffered all things, He now became perfect. He had overcome temptations, He had restored the gospel, established His Church, and now suffered death to come upon Him "to fulfill all righteousness" (Matthew 3:15), that He might inaugurate the wholly new program of the Resurrection, so mysterious and unexplainable to the people. ("The Greatest Miracle," *Relief Society Magazine,* April 1947, 219)

Jesus of Nazareth came into the world to bring to pass the Atonement, which gives to all men everywhere immortality through the gift of the resurrection. Thus Jesus' teachings can clearly help us to live a righteous life and to be happier here, but

His great sacrifice guarantees to us immortality and the extension of our individual identity and life beyond the grave. ("The Abundant Life," *Ensign,* July 1978, 3)

In God's divine plan, provision was made for a redeemer to break the bonds of death and, through the resurrection, make possible the reunion of the spirits and bodies of all persons who had dwelt on earth. Jesus of Nazareth was the one who, before the world was created, was chosen to come to earth to perform this service, to conquer mortal death. This voluntary action would atone for the fall of Adam and Eve and permit the spirit of man to recover his body, thereby reuniting body and spirit. ("The True Way of Life and Salvation," *Ensign,* May 1978, 4)

Only a God could bring about this miracle of resurrection. As a teacher of righteousness, Jesus could inspire souls to goodness; as a prophet, He could foreshadow the future; as an intelligent leader of men, He could organize a church; and as a possessor and magnifier of the priesthood, He could heal the sick, give sight to the blind, even raise other dead; but only as a God could He raise Himself from the tomb, overcome death permanently, and bring incorruption in place of corruption, and replace mortality with immortality. . . .

And so we bear testimony that the Being who created the earth and its contents, who made numerous appearances upon the earth prior to His birth in Bethlehem, Jesus Christ, the Son of God, is resurrected and immortal, and that this great boon of resurrection and immortality becomes now, through our Redeemer, the heritage of mankind. ("The Greatest Miracle," *Relief Society Magazine,* April 1947, 219)

This resurrection referred to is the work of Jesus Christ, the Savior, who, because He was both mortal (the son of Mary) and divine (the Son of God), was able to overcome the powers governing the flesh. He actually gave His life and literally took it up again as the "first fruits," to be followed by every soul that has ever lived. Being a god, He gave His life. No one could take it from Him. He had developed, through His perfection in overcoming all things, the power to take up His life again. Death was His last enemy, and He overcame even that and established the resurrection. This is an absolute truth. All the theorists in the world cannot disprove it. It is a fact. (Written for April 1977 General Conference)

REVELATION

A new truth, a concept not understood by the myriads of people on the earth, burst forth, and in that moment there was only one man on the face of the whole earth who knew with absolute assurance that God was a personal being, that the Father and Son were separate individuals with bodies of flesh and bones, [and that he] had been created in their image. (Meeting for investigators, Tempe, Arizona, 7 June 1974)

This Church has as its foundation the principle of revelation. There were many organizations already in the world which had been organized by good men of understanding and spirituality—many churches planned by good men. The only justification for another church to come forth in 1830 was that the true church must be restored; a church that would come from the Lord Jesus Christ; it would have to be His church that would teach His doctrines by His authority and through revelation. (BYU Stake Conference, 13 Jan. 1957)

Logic is the father of hundreds of sects; it is the mother of the great apostasy. Revelation is the rock and the Lord has given us the key above. By faith do the will of the Father, and the knowledge follows. (Letter dated 31 May 1948)

He has given the key. You may know. You need not be in doubt. Follow the prescribed procedures, and you may have an absolute knowledge that these things are absolute truths. The necessary procedure is: study, think, pray, and do. Revelation is the key. God will make it known to you once you have capitulated and have become humble and receptive. Having dropped all pride of your mental stature, having acknowledged before God your confusion, having subjected your egotism and having surrendered yourself to the teaching of the Holy Spirit, you are ready to begin to learn. With preconceived religious notions stubbornly held, one is not teachable. The Lord has promised repeatedly that He will give you a knowledge of spiritual things when you have placed yourself in a proper frame of mind. He has counseled us to seek, ask, and search diligently. These innumerable promises are epitomized by Moroni in the following: "And by the power of the Holy Ghost ye may know the truth of all things." (Moroni 10:5.) What a promise! ("Absolute Truth," *Ensign,* Sept. 1978, 3)

For many it seems difficult to accept as revelation those numerous messages . . . which come to prophets as deep, unassailable impressions settling down on the prophet's mind and heart as dew from heaven or as the dawn displaces the darkness of night.

Many men seem to have no ear for spiritual messages nor comprehension of them when they come in common dress.

Expecting the spectacular, one may not be fully alerted to the constant flow of revealed communication. (Munich Area Conference, 26 Aug. 1973)

Revelation has not ceased and will not cease. This kingdom of God has been set up for the rest of time, never to be torn down nor given to another people. It is a continuous program and will grow instead of diminish. Its doctrines are well established, but because of growth and expansion, improved ways are afforded to teach the gospel all over the world. Additional servants are called to the increasing work for a bigger world. Revelation and other miracles will never cease unless faith ceases. ("Continuing Revelation," *Ensign*, Feb. 1971, 20)

The restored Church of Jesus Christ is founded upon the rock of revelation. Continuous revelation is indeed the very lifeblood of the gospel of the living Lord and Savior, Jesus Christ. How this confused world of today needs revelation from God! ("Revelation: The Word of the Lord to His Prophets," *Ensign*, May 1977, 76)

When a new temple is projected, when a new mission is organized, when stakes are divided and vital vacancies are filled, there is certainty and calm, tranquil assurance, and the peace of heaven settles over the hearts of true believers with a sureness. Even great and good men rise to new stature under the mantle of prime authority when keys of heaven are closed in their palms and then the voice of authority comes from their lips. ("'To His Servants the Prophets,'" *Instructor,* Aug. 1960, 256)

When man begins to hunger, when arms begin to reach, when knees begin to bend and voices begin to articulate, then, and not until then, does the Lord make Himself known. He pushes back the horizons, He breaks the curtain above us, and He makes it possible for us to come out of dim, uncertain stumbling into the sureness of the eternal light. (Santiago Area Conference, 1 March 1977)

One woman claimed she was receiving revelations every day while putting up the lunches in the temple. The purported revelations were childish and silly and pertained to such little things as the Lord would never deign to control or guide. At first I said, "These are not from the Lord. He does not deal with these little things where we can make up our own minds, such as what clothes to wear or what to eat today." My observation to her did not do any good. Her "revelations" came all the more, and she knew they were from the Lord. Then I said to her, "Well, now, sister, if these come from the Lord, they are for you alone. Do not ever whisper them to a soul." When she quit telling about them, they ceased to come anymore. She was just glorying in her superiority over her fellow beings when she received them. . . . If one does receive revelations, which one may expect if he is worthy, they will always be in total alignment with the program of the Church; they will never be counter. And they will always be within his own jurisdiction and never beyond. ("The Ordinances of the Gospel," BYU, 18 June 1962)

REVERENCE

We must remember that reverence is not a somber, temporary behavior that we adopt on Sunday. True reverence involves happiness, as well as love, respect, gratitude, and godly fear. It is a virtue that should be part of our way of life. In fact, Latter-day Saints should be the most reverent people in all the earth. ("We Should Be a Reverent People," pamphlet, 1976)

As we quietly enter the door of the chapel we may leave behind us outside all criticisms, worries, and cares—all occupational, political, social, and recreational plans—and calmly give ourselves to contemplation and to worship. We may bathe in the spiritual atmosphere. We may devote ourselves to learning, repenting, forgiving, testifying, appreciating, and loving. (Letter, undated)

SABBATH

In my extensive travels I find many faithful people who forego the Sabbath day profits and those which come from the handling of the forbidden things. I have found cattle communities where the stockmen never carry on their roundup on the Sabbath; fruit stands along the roadside which are open night and day, but which close on Sunday even in the short fruit season; drugstores and confectionery businesses which earn their money on the six weekdays; eating houses and wayside stands, closed on the Lord's day. And there are many other people who might rationalize and justify themselves in Sunday profit taking but who take satisfaction and joy in refraining. And every time I see good folk who are willing to forego these profits, I rejoice and feel within my heart to bless them for their steadfastness, their courage, and their faith. ("Keep Your Money Clean," *Improvement Era,* Dec. 1953, 226)

The Sabbath is a day on which to take inventory—to analyze our weaknesses, to confess our sins to our associates and our Lord. It is a day on which to fast in "sackcloth and ashes." It is a day on which to read good books, a day to contemplate and ponder, a day to study lessons for priesthood and auxiliary organizations, a day to study the scriptures and to prepare sermons, a day to nap and rest and relax, a day to visit the sick, a day to preach the gospel, a day to proselyte, a day to visit quietly with the family and get acquainted with our children, a day for proper courting, a day to do good, a day to drink at the fountain of knowledge and of instruction, a day to seek forgiveness of our sins, a day for the enrichment of our spirit and our soul, a day to restore us to our spiritual stature, a day to partake of the emblems of His sacrifice and atonement, a day to contemplate the glories of the gospel and of the eternal realms, a day to climb high on the upward path toward our Heavenly Father. . . .

The observance of the Sabbath is a part of the new covenant. ("The Fourth Commandment," *M Man-Gleaner Manual,* 1963–64, 265)

SACRAMENT MEETING

We attend sacrament meetings to worship the Lord. If the meeting is conducted or if we attend with any other thought, we have missed the spirit of the occasion. . . . The best choir, the best speaker, the most noted lecturer, cannot bring true worship into your soul. It must proceed from within, out of a deep sense of love and devotion and dependence and humility. . . .

Because the speaker is local, or dry, is a poor excuse for not attending meetings, though it is often given. How very weak! If you sing and pray and partake of the sacrament worthily, you could sit through the next hour in worshipful contemplation with profit even if the speaker is poor. It is your responsibility to make the meeting worthwhile by your individual contribution. The average ward has in it many talented and forceful speakers. They should be used. They should be encouraged to fill their minds with useful knowledge so that their message and testimony will be of great value when they are called on. The Lord has never agreed to bring finished sermons from empty minds and hearts, but He has covenanted that He will bring to your remembrance the things you have learned. (Written for General Conference April 1945)

We do not go to Sabbath meetings to be entertained or even solely to be instructed. We go to worship the Lord. It is an individual responsibility, and regardless of what is said from the pulpit, if one wishes to worship the Lord in spirit and in truth, he may do so by attending his meetings, partaking of the sacrament, and contemplating the beauties of the gospel. If the service is a failure to you, you have failed. No one can worship for you; you must do your own waiting upon the Lord. ("The Sabbath—A Delight," *Ensign,* Jan. 1978, 2)

SACRIFICE

Sacrifice brings forth the blessings of heaven. And when we get away from sacrifice in all of our Church work, in our service and in the organizations and the subsidiaries, I tell you, when we get away from the sacrifice, we have slipped a cog.

Sacrifices for a just cause make character. ("Lengthening Our Stride," Regional Representatives Conference, 3 Oct. 1974)

SATAN

In these days of sophistication and error men depersonalize not only God but the devil. Under this concept Satan is a myth, useful for keeping people straight in less enlightened days but outmoded in our educated age. Nothing is further from reality. Satan is very much a personal, individual spirit being, but without a mortal body. His desires to seal each of us his are no less ardent in wickedness than our Father's are in righteousness to attract us to His own eternal kingdom. (*Miracle,* 21)

The adversary is so smart and subtle that he takes every man in his own game. The man whose weakness is money will be led inch by inch and yard by yard and mile by mile into that area where his wants can be satisfied. If one's ambition is power, the evil one knows exactly how to build him up to that point. If one's weakness is sex, Satan in his erudition and experience and brilliance knows a thousand reasons why sex may be liberated to run rampant and express itself and satisfy itself. Lucifer is real. He is subtle. He is convincing. He is powerful. (Letter dated 28 Feb. 1966)

SCRIPTURE

I ask us all to honestly evaluate our performance in scripture study. It is a common thing to have a few passages of scripture at our disposal, floating in our minds, as it were, and thus to have the illusion that we know a great deal about the gospel. In this sense, having a little knowledge can be a problem indeed. I am convinced that each of us, at some time in our lives, must discover the scriptures for ourselves—and not just discover them once, but rediscover them again and again. ("How Rare a Possession—The Scriptures!" *Ensign,* Sept. 1976, 2)

In the careful, regular, and systematic study of the standard works of the Church will be found the material for a lifetime of profitable study.

Here are the pictures of people who lived and met all the exigencies of life and overcame meanness, jealousies, envies, hatreds, and became pure of heart and clean of hands. Here are pictures of the winds of disobedience and rebellion and uncleanness and the whirlwinds that enveloped them. Here are men who approached perfection under trials and difficulties, like Job, and who emerged superior beings. Here are the biographies of the prophets and of leaders and of the Lord himself, giving example and direction so that men can, by following those examples, be perfected, happy, full of joy, and with eternity their goal and expectation. . . .

In all the commentaries [by general authorities], good as they may be, it must be remembered that none takes the place of the original source material. ("The Power of Books," *Relief Society Magazine,* Oct. 1963, 724)

I find that when I get casual in my relationships with divinity and when it seems that no divine ear is listening and no divine voice is speaking, that I am far, far away. If I immerse myself in the scriptures the distance narrows and the spirituality returns. I find myself loving more intensely those whom I must love with all my heart and mind and strength, and loving them more, I find it easier to abide their counsel. ("What I Hope You Will Teach My Grandchildren," BYU Seminary and Institute Teachers Conference, 11 July 1966)

Study the scriptures. Thus you may gain strength through the understanding of eternal things. You young women need this close relationship with the mind and will of our Eternal Father. We want our sisters to be scholars of the scriptures as well as our men. ("Privileges and Responsibilities of Sisters," *Ensign,* Nov. 1978, 102)

Remember in the Book of Mormon the promise is given that on certain conditions God "will manifest the truth of it unto you, by the power of the Holy Ghost. And by the power of the Holy Ghost ye may know the truth of all things." [Moroni

10:4–5.] Such a testimony is not promised to anyone who reads the book with a critical attitude nor to one who reads it to satisfy curiosity nor to one who resists it, but definitely it will come to everyone who has fully surrendered himself with an open mind and heart. And when this testimony comes to readers it is quite unlikely that it will come by flourish of trumpets or by handwriting on the wall or by audible voice, but by a burning of hearts in bosoms. (Letter dated 6 March 1947)

SELF-RELIANCE

With regard to all phases of our lives, I believe that men should help themselves. They should plow and plant and cultivate and harvest and not expect their faith to bring them bread. (Beneficial Life convention, Snowmass, Colorado, Aug. 1974)

Maintain a year's supply. The Lord has urged that His people save for the rainy days, prepare for the difficult times, and put away for emergencies a year's supply or more of bare necessities so that when comes the flood, the earthquake, the famine, the hurricane, the storms of life, our families can be sustained through the dark days. ("Who Contendeth With the Almighty," written for the Manchester Area Conference, Aug. 1971)

SERVICE

God does notice us, and He watches over us. But it is usually through another mortal that He meets our needs. Therefore, it is vital that we serve each other in the kingdom. . . .

So often, our acts of service consist of simple encouragement or of giving mundane help with mundane tasks—but what glorious consequences can flow from mundane acts and from small but deliberate deeds! ("Small Acts of Service," *Ensign,* Dec. 1974, 2)

Helping others live the gospel is service. One has hardly proved his life abundant until he has built up a crumbling wall, paid off a heavy debt, enticed a disbeliever to his knees, filled an empty stomach, influenced a soul to wash in the blood of the Lamb, turned fear and frustration into peace and sureness, led one to be "born again."

One is measuring up to his opportunity potential when he has saved a crumbling marriage, transformed the weak into the strong, changed a civil to a proper temple marriage, brought enemies from the cesspool of hate to the garden of love, made a child trust and love him, changed a scoffer into a worshiper, melted a stony heart into one of flesh and muscle. ("How to Evaluate Your Performance," *Improvement Era,* Nov. 1969, 22)

Most of us have little influence on world affairs. If we can make a contribution to peace on a large scale, we should do so; but our first task is to regulate our own lives properly and to care for our families and our neighbors before we go too far afield.

There is no end of potential causes to which you can devote your time and talents and treasure. Be careful to select good causes. (*Speaks,* 40–41)

The Lord is just as pleased with any soul on this earth who magnifies whatever calling the Lord has given him as He is with those whose lives and accomplishments are more visible. President J. Reuben Clark, Jr., said simply but eloquently, "In the service of the Lord, it is not where you serve but how. In The Church of Jesus Christ of Latter-day Saints, one takes the place to which one is duly called, which place one neither seeks nor declines." ("Integrity: The Spirit of BYU," BYU, 4 Sept. 1979)

Before being baptized the new convert should understand that this Church is like a beehive, and that activity earns the rewards of heaven, and that just believing will not take one far in his quest toward exaltation. ("The Image of a Stake," Regional Representatives Conference, 4 Oct. 1973)

None of us should become so busy in our formal Church assignments that there is no room left for quiet Christian service to our neighbors. (Temple View Area Conference, 21 Feb. 1976)

Perhaps you could take a loaf of bread or a covered dish to someone in need. Uncompensated service is one good answer to overcoming loneliness. (Special Interest fireside, 29 Dec. 1974)

I would hope that you who are training to be teachers would not be learning to teach for the compensation that would come each month, but that you might inspire people throughout your lifetime, that you might build faith and build character in many. I would hope that you who are following other fields of endeavor, that your education and your employment would be a means to an end and not the end in and of itself. . . . Do great things for the glory of God and for the benefit of mankind. ("Miracles," BYU, 11 Feb. 1947)

I know a man who has never given thought to himself. His every desire was for the protection and pleasure of those about him. No task was too great, no sacrifice too much for him to make for his fellowmen. His means brought relief from physical suffering; his kind work and thoughtfulness brought comfort and cheer and courage.

Wherever people were in distress, he was on hand, cheering the discouraged, burying the dead, comforting the bereaved, and proving himself a friend in need. His time, his means, and his energies were lavished upon those needing assistance. Having given himself freely, by that same act he has added to his mental, physical, and moral stature until today he stands in his declining years a power for good, an example and an inspiration to many. He has developed and grown until he is everywhere acclaimed, loved, and appreciated. He has given life and in a real way has truly found the abundant life. ("The Abundant Life," Safford High School commencement, Safford, Arizona, 1939)

SIN

There is no tragedy except in sin. Let us know therefore that life is eternal, and that God doeth all things well; and this righteous son, the offspring of God, was not born for a day, a decade, or a century, but for eternity. Only his own lack of righteousness could ever deprive him of any blessing promised by the Lord. Thy son liveth and continues to radiate life, not death; light, not darkness; commencement, not termination; assurance, not uncertainty; joy eternal, not sorrow; sweetness, not bitterness; youthful maturity, not senility; progress, not stoppage; sunshine, not clouds; clearness of vision, not confusion and dimness; fulfillment, not frustration; an open gate with light ahead, not barred windows with darkness beyond. ("'Thy Son Liveth,'" *Improvement Era*, May 1945, 253)

Whoever said that sin was not fun? Whoever claimed that Lucifer was not handsome, persuasive, easy, friendly? Whoever said that sin was unattractive, undesirable, or nauseating in its acceptance?

Transgression wears elegant gowns and sparkling apparel. It is highly perfumed, has attractive features, a soft voice. It is found in educated circles and sophisticated groups. It provides sweet and comfortable luxuries. Sin is easy and has a big company of bedfellows. It promises immunity from restrictions, temporary freedoms. It can momentarily satisfy hunger, thirst, desire, urges, passions, wants, without immediately paying the price. But, it begins tiny and grows to monumental proportions. It grows drop by drop, inch by inch. ("The False Gods We Worship," *Ensign*, June 1976, 3)

The Church and its agencies and institutions constitute a little island in a great ocean. If we cannot hold the line and keep the floods of error and sin from entangling us and engulfing us, there is little hope for the world. Tidal waves of corruption, evil, deceit, and dishonor are pounding our shores constantly. Unless we can build breakwaters and solid walls to hold them back, the sea will engulf us and destroy us also. ("What I Hope You Will Teach My Grandchildren," BYU Seminary and Institute Teacher Conference, 11 July 1966)

TEACHING

Above all, I hope you will teach faith in the living God and in His Only Begotten Son—not a superficial, intellectual kind of acceptance, but a deep, spiritual, inner feeling of dependence and closeness; not a fear composed of panic and terror, but a fear of the Lord composed mostly of intense love and admiration and awesome nearness in a relationship of parent and offspring—father and son—father and daughter. ("What I Hope You Will Teach My Grandchildren," BYU Seminary and Institute Teacher Conference, 11 July 1966)

TEMPLE

It seems to me it would be a fine thing if every set of parents would have in every bedroom in their house a picture of the temple so the boy or girl from the time he is an infant could look at the picture every day and it becomes a part of his life. When he reaches the age that he needs to make this very important decision, it will have already been made. ("The Matter of Marriage," University of Utah Institute of Religion, 22 Oct. 1976)

Holy temples may also be defiled and desecrated by members of the Church who go into the temple and make covenants unworthily or which they are not prepared or willing to accept and carry forward. When people go to the temple and then make light of its sacred principles, they are defiling it. When unrepentant people accept the holy ordinances without full determination to prove worthy of them, they are helping to violate the sacredness of the holy temple and they are desecrating holy places. ("The Things of Eternity— Stand We in Jeopardy?" *Ensign,* Jan. 1977, 3)

The temples are reserved for sacred ordinances pertaining to the living and the dead. Worthy members of the Church should go to the temples as often as possible to participate in this important work. One of the ordinances performed in the temple is that of the endowment, which comprises a course of instruction relating to the eternal journey of a man and woman from the pre-earthly existence through the earthly experience and on to the exaltation each may attain. ("The Things of Eternity—Stand We in Jeopardy?" *Ensign,* Jan. 1977, 3)

Together you [the Lamanites] and we shall build in the spectacular city of New Jerusalem the temple to which our Redeemer will come. Your hands with ours, also those of Jacob, will place the foundation stones, raise the walls, and roof the magnificent structure. Perhaps your artistic hands will paint the temple and decorate it with a master's touch, and together we shall dedicate to our Creator Lord the most beautiful of all temples ever built to his name. ("To You . . . Our Kinsmen," *Improvement Era,* Dec. 1959, 938)

TEMPTATION

Temptation is like Goliath. Now, my young brothers, remember that every David has a Goliath to defeat, and every Goliath can be defeated. He may not be a bully who fights with fists or sword or gun. He may not even be flesh and blood. He may not be nine feet tall; he may not be armor-protected, but every boy has his Goliaths. And every boy has access to the brook with its smooth stones.

You will meet Goliaths who threaten you. Whether your Goliath is a town bully or is the temptation to steal or to destroy or the temptation to rob or the desire to curse and swear; if your Goliath is the desire to wantonly destroy or the temptation to lust and to sin, or the urge to avoid activity, whatever is your Goliath, he can be slain. But remember, to be the victor, one must follow the path that David followed: "David behaved himself wisely in all his ways; and the Lord was with him." (1 Samuel 18:14.) ("The Davids and the Goliaths," *Ensign,* Nov. 1974, 79)

This is our proper pattern, if we would prevent sin rather than be faced with the much more difficult task of curing it. As I study the story of the Redeemer and His temptations, I am certain He spent His energies fortifying himself against temptation rather than battling with it to conquer it. (*Miracle,* 215–17)

We are faced with powerful forces unleashed by the adversary. Waves of sin—they come with great power and speed, and they will catch us if we are unwary. But a warning is sounded for us. It behooves us to listen to the warning and to flee from evil for our eternal lives. We cannot stand against them unaided. It is not the brave man, but the fool, who stands against forces more powerful than he. We must flee to the safety of high ground, where the wave cannot reach us; or, if that is not possible, we must hold fast to that which can keep us from being swept away. Even if we are inundated let us hold our breath and keep a firm grasp on that which can save us. (Independence Missouri Stake Center dedication, 3 Sept. 1978)

Every thought that one permits through his mind leaves its trace. Thoughts are things. Our lives are governed a great deal by our thoughts. (Brisbane Area Conference, 1 March 1976)

TESTIMONY

And now may I write what I cannot speak, that through the silent hours I have had a chance to weigh, and ponder, and evaluate, and through all these experiences my vision has been expanded, my love deepened, my determinations to grow more like our Savior increased and my knowledge fortified that mortality is but one important incident in life, that the plan of salvation and exaltation is a positive reality, that our Lord speaks constantly from the heavens, that this is His work, that we are His unprofitable servants and that the rewards are sure. That is the way it is. That I know. (Remarks to the Council of the Twelve, 10 April 1957)

Do not exhort each other; that is not a testimony. Do not tell others how to live. Just tell how you feel inside. That is the testimony. The moment you begin preaching to others, your testimony ends. Just tell us how you feel, what your mind and heart and every fiber of your body tells you. (Berlin Mission Conference, 15 Jan. 1962)

Everything has to be fed. You feed your body three times a day. The Lord says to keep your testimony, to keep your spirit alive, you have to feed it every day. That is why He says pray morning, noon, and night. That is why He says pray continually so that you keep that line open. (Cordoba Missionary Conference, 17 Nov. 1966)

I add my own testimony. I know that Jesus Christ is the Son of the living God and that He was crucified for the sins of the world. He is my friend, my Savior, my Lord, my God. ("An Eternal Hope in Christ," *Ensign,* Nov. 1978, 71)

In courts of law the witness is asked to take an
oath that the information he is about to give is
"the truth, the whole truth, and nothing but the
truth," and the statements made are called his
"testimony." In spiritual matters, we may likewise
have a testimony. This sureness of the spiritual is
unique and pertains to the realness of a personal
God; the continued active life of the Christ, separate from but like His Father; the divinity of the
restoration of the organization and doctrines of
God's church on the earth and the power of the
divine, authoritative priesthood given to men,
through revelations from God. These can be
known as surely as that the sun shines, by every
responsible person, and to fail to attain this
knowledge is to admit that one has not paid the
price. ("Are You a Modern Nicodemus?"
Improvement Era, June 1958, 148)

Knowing full well that before long, in the natural
course of events, I must stand before the Lord and
give an accounting of my words, I now add my
personal and solemn testimony that God, the
Eternal Father, and the risen Lord, Jesus Christ,
appeared to the boy Joseph Smith. I testify that
the Book of Mormon is a translation of an
ancient record of nations who once lived in this
western hemisphere, where they prospered and
became mighty when they kept the command-

ments of God, but who were largely destroyed through terrible civil wars when they forgot God. This book bears testimony of the living reality of the Lord Jesus Christ as the Savior and Redeemer of mankind.

I testify that the holy priesthood, both Aaronic and Melchizedek with authority to act in the name of God, was restored to the earth by John the Baptist, and Peter, James, and John; that other keys and authority were subsequently restored; and that the power and authority of those various divine bestowals are among us today. Of these things I bear solemn witness to all within the sound of my voice. I promise in the name of the Lord that all who give heed to our message, and accept and live the gospel, will grow in faith and understanding. They will have an added measure of peace in their lives and in their homes and by the power of the Holy Ghost will speak similar words of testimony and truth. I do this and leave my blessing upon you in the name of Jesus Christ. Amen. (Dedication of buildings in Fayette, New York, *Ensign,* May 1980, 54)

Testimony is the electric light illuminating the cavern; the wind and sun dissipating the fog; the power equipment removing boulders from the road. It is the mansion on the hill replacing the shack in the marshes; the harvester shelving the sickle and cradle; the tractor, train, automobile, and plane displacing the ox team. It is the rich, nourishing kernels of corn instead of the husks in the trough. It is much more than all else, for "this is life eternal, that they might know thee the only true God, and Jesus Christ whom thou hast sent." (John 17:3.) ("Are You a Modern Nicodemus?" *Improvement Era,* June 1958, 148)

The darkest day in all a man's life or eternity is not when he is physically injured or suffers untimely death, but that day when the fire for lack of proper fuel dies down and flickers and sputters and goes out. I repeat—the saddest hour of any man's eternity is when his rationalizations put out his fires and leave them but embers. (Letter dated 28 Feb. 1966)

THANKFULNESS

Even in our prayers, our words are mostly *gimme*—"Father, make us strong, give us health, make us righteous"—when we should be thanking Him mostly and asking only for help in our doing these things for ourselves. ("'Whatsoever Things Are Honest,'" BYU, June 1958)

THRIFT

I am not howling calamity, but I fear that a great majority of our young people, never having known calamity, depression, hunger, homelessness, joblessness, cannot conceive of such situations ever coming again. There are thousands of young families in this city who could not stand without suffering a three-month period without income. They might find their home being foreclosed, their car repossessed, their electric and home equipment being taken back, and themselves being reduced to unbelievable rations in the necessities.

The great difficulty is that when difficult times come, those who in normal times could lend assistance are also under the wheel of the grinding mill. It may be impossible to anticipate and prepare for the eventualities of depression, war, invasion, bombing, but we can go a long way. What I have seen with my own eyes makes me afraid not to do what I can to protect against the calamities. . . . You have what you think is adequate insurance, but are you prepared for and protected against death, illness, a long-continuing, crippling illness of the breadwinner? How long can you go if the income stops? What are your reserves? How long could you make your many payments on home, car, implements, appliances?

How long could you carry armloads of groceries from a cash store? (Letter, undated)

I had an experience once with a man whose wife was leaving him, taking their three little girls. He lost his position, his membership in the Church was in jeopardy, and he was deeply in debt and being "hounded" (as he called it) by collectors. Suicide was in his mind. I told him I would help him if he would cooperate. With reluctance he gave me a list of his long-past-due accounts. The collectors were threatening. There were payments on the house, car, furniture, clothes, gasoline, and tires. He owed the grocer, the barber, the music store, the drugstore, and the utility companies. I found him a job but it would pay only eighty dollars a month. He got himself a modest room with an electric plate. He was to fry his own eggs and eat a simple supper and buy one wholesome meal a day without desserts. He was to store the car in a yard and walk to work and church. Then we budgeted.

First there was eight dollars for tithing, for how could he ever expect to have the blessings of the Lord without showing his faith? Twenty-five dollars was to go to one creditor, fifteen dollars to another, five dollars or three dollars or fifty cents to another in proportion to the size of the accounts. At my insistence he went to these creditors and explained his helplessness, his income from this temporary job, and what he could do by way of liquidating the due amount. To his surprise all those whom he thought were tough and mean agreed to his plan. On each payday we allocated the funds. He met smiling faces, kindly people eager to assist one who was really trying. The money was not his. It belonged to his creditors to whom he had promised it. He thought I was tough when I cut out his shine money and told him to buy a box of shoe polish and shine his shoes like I did mine. He was surprised when I insisted on newspaper money going to his creditors. "Where you work, they take the newspaper. You can take the day-old copy home with you after it is discarded." He was a good sport, cooperative, and his countenance shone as he began to see himself coming out of the hole and becoming master of the situation. A few months went by and the smaller accounts were cleared away and larger payments were made to the larger ones. His walking to work and church and eating only wholesome foods gave him new vigor; his visit to the bishop every week brought him a new association pleasant to him; his feeling of triumph of being master of his destiny gave him a lighter step. He found a better job with twice the income. The creditors smiled as the payments increased. Not until all old accounts were squared did he move to a better apartment and put gas in his car. ("'Whatsoever Things Are Honest,'" BYU, June 1958)

TITHING

A chapel is needed in South Africa, and to the smaller amount subscribed by the local members, there comes from the tithing reservoir the larger amount to pay for the edifice. In Chicago or Macon or Tucson or Missoula, or in any other of the thousands of branches and wards, the accumulated funds from the reservoir come to bring blessings which otherwise would be out of reach for the individual community. A temple is needed in Europe for the tens of thousands who cannot travel nor emigrate to the United States, and a channel is opened and cooperative funds flow to build, equip, and administer a temple there.

A school is required for young Mexicans, otherwise deprived, and the reservoir is tapped, and buildings are constructed, teachers employed, and youth trained.

A fertile field for proselyting develops in a foreign country, another faucet is turned, and wealth is drawn to buy property, establish a mission home, and pay return fares for the numerous missionaries who also, in a great cooperative effort, proselyte and bring thousands into the Church yearly.

And numerous Church projects are made possible by mass effort which would not be possible to each individual.

Thus from the widow in Ogden, the little child in Finland, the young Lamanite convert in Guatemala, the rich man of New York, the newsboy in Seattle, the blind woman of New Zealand come the funds in pennies and pesos, francs, and marks for the numerous progressive and productive projects of a great organization involving a million and a half people—all by cooperation of effort. ("The Spirit of Co-operation," *Improvement Era,* Sept. 1957, 632)

It is the uncompensated things we do from a spirit of unselfishness which bring us uplift and satisfaction and growth. Little exultation is experienced when one pays his taxes, for he here has no choice; but when one pays his tithing with a grateful heart for the privilege and no one knows but himself and the bishop, and no acclaim or publicity or worldly renown is given him, he is compensated in the feeling that he has "measured up"—that he has kept faith with his faith. (Letter dated 29 Oct. 1947)

The tithing principle is a solution for poverty. The cure to poverty lies in Isaiah fifty-eighth chapter and in Malachi third chapter: "Bring ye all the tithes into the storehouse, that there may be meat in mine house."

I hear voices asking in insolence and wonder and disbelief: "How can a scripture solve poverty and want?" Then I quote further: "And prove me now herewith, saith the Lord of hosts, if I will not open you the windows of heaven, and pour you out a blessing, that there shall not be room enough to receive it." (Malachi 3:10.)

Ah! That is what we need across the tracks, in India and Pakistan, in our big cities, in disadvantaged countries—to have the heavens open.

Apparently earth has not provided the answer; now shall we try heaven? The Lord has promised to open the windows of heaven. ("The Gospel Solves Problems of the World," BYU 10-Stake Fireside, 26 Sept. 1971)

When I was a boy, I used to put up hay. I would drive the horses that were hitched to the wagon and tramp the hay down and my older brothers pitched it on the wagon, and when we had gone to the field in the morning, my father would say, "Now, boys, this is the tenth load this morning. This belongs to the Lord. You go up into the upper part where the hay is the best and get a big load and then take it over to the big barn in which the bishop keeps the Church hay." In that way I learned how to pay tithing, so it isn't hard for me to obey this law. ("Teach Children," Pachuca Mexico Stake Conference, 2 Nov. 1952)

TOLERANCE

While there is an ever-increasing number of people who are kind and willing to accept the minority groups as they come into the Church, there are still many who speak in disparaging terms, who priest-like and Levite-like pass by on the other side of the street. . . .

The Lord would have eliminated bigotry and class distinction. He talked to the Samaritan woman at the well, healed the centurion's kin, and blessed the child of the Canaanitish woman. And though He personally came to the "lost sheep of the house of Israel" and sent His apostles first to them rather than to the Samaritans and other Gentiles, yet He later sent Paul to bring the gospel to the Gentiles and revealed to Peter that the gospel was for all. ("The Evil of Intolerance," *Improvement Era,* June 1954, 423)

The most lovable quality any human being can possess is tolerance. It is the vision that enables one to see things from another's viewpoint. It is the generosity that concedes to others the right to their own opinions and peculiarities. It is the bigness that enables us to let people be happy in their own way instead of our way. (Funeral of Janie Pace, Safford, Arizona, 1943)

UNITY

A united group has great influence. I come to realize more and more, as my experience broadens, the vast influence and power that a small minority may wield in this world, in politics, in religion, in social activities, everywhere you go. A small group, united in purpose, with definite goals, may greatly influence the great majorities. ("The Florescence of the Lamanites," *Relief Society Magazine,* Feb. 1953, 76)

VALUES

Old values are upheld by the Church not because they are old, but rather because through the ages they have proved right. It will always be the rule. ("President Kimball Speaks Out on Morality," *Ensign,* Nov. 1980, 94)

VANDALISM

When I lived in Arizona as a boy, nearly all the farmers had melon patches, and some of the farmers raised them for the market. Sometimes some boys would gang up and in the darkness of the night, go to one of these melon patches, and with their jackknives go through the patch and slash all the melons they could reach. They did not want the melons to eat, merely an ugly, destructive urge to destroy. This I never could understand, and I could never understand setting fire to things or breaking windows or tearing rugs or any of the mean tricks that were destructive in nature. ("The Davids and the Goliaths," *Ensign,* Nov. 1974, 79)

WAR

The precipitous walls on the high hills of Jerusalem deflected for a time the arrows and spears of enemies, the catapults and firebrands. But even then wickedness did not lessen, men did not learn lessons. Hunger scaled the walls; thirst broke down the gates; immorality, cannibalism, idolatry, godlessness stalked about till destruction came. ("Listen to the Prophet's Voice," *Improvement Era,* Dec. 1961, 936)

Though food be scarce, and starvation stalks abroad, men will still share their portion, give succor to the afflicted, sympathy to the bereaved, and help to the unfortunate. Though cities be bombed, families separated, the meaning of sympathy and understanding and brotherhood will not change. Courage is not dead, ambition is not slain, love is not replaced. The bombed cities shall rise again, the grain that was burned shall be replanted, the fountain that evil has polluted shall flow pure again, the battered forests will shoot forth new foliage and the grass will spring forth anew to obliterate the traces of war. Even though a thousand times they shall afflict the earth, a thousand times will it come forth again and men will survive to plant the ground and build upon it. The conditions of life in this chaotic situation are changed, but the meaning of the fundamentals of life have not changed. (Funeral of Janie Pace, Safford, Arizona, 1943)

We are a warlike people, easily distracted from our assignment of preparing for the coming of the Lord. When enemies rise up, we commit vast resources to the fabrication of gods of stone and steel—ships, planes, missiles, fortifications—and depend on them for protection and deliverance. When threatened, we become anti-enemy instead of pro-kingdom of God; we train a man in the art of war and call him a patriot, thus, in the manner of Satan's counterfeit of true patriotism, perverting the Savior's teaching:

"Love your enemies, bless them that curse you, do good to them that hate you, and pray for them which despitefully use you, and persecute you;

"That ye may be the children of your Father which is in heaven." (Matthew 5:44–45.)

We forget that if we are righteous the Lord will either not suffer our enemies to come upon us—and this is the special promise to the inhabitants of the land of the Americas—or He will fight our battles for us. . . .

What are we to fear when the Lord is with us? Can we not take the Lord at His word and exercise a particle of faith in Him? ("The False Gods We Worship," *Ensign*, June 1976, 3)

When armies march and people fight, education suffers, art languishes, buildings crumble, forests are exploited, farms return to desert, and orchards to jungle. Fighting men build temporary bridges, forts, and towers instead of homes, public buildings, and observatories. There is neither time nor inclination to carve statues, paint landscapes, compose music, or record history. Communities on the march or in retreat have no schools nor teachers. Priceless records are destroyed with the buildings and cities which are burned and pillaged. Artists, scholars, writers, and clergy alike shoulder arms, stalking enemies, and laying siege to cities. Plunder replaces honest industry. Cattle, goats, and poultry are devoured by voracious soldiers. Calves, kids, and piglets are eaten, as are the seed-corn and the wheat. Fruit is devoured, and trees are burned for wood. Today's insatiable hunger swallows tomorrow's plenty. Armies carry movable tents and abandon homes and churches. Temples fall in ruins and are overgrown by vegetation. Life becomes a sordid existence, bloody, with little purpose except to survive. . . . Long and bloody wars mean sacked, burned, ruined cities, confiscatory taxes, degenerated peoples, and decayed cultures.

Victory and defeat alike leave countries devastated and the conqueror and the conquered reduced. Wickedness brings war, and war vomits destruction and suffering, hate and bloodshed upon the guilty and the innocent. ("The Book of Vital Messages," *Improvement Era,* June 1963, 490)

It seems almost a hopeless undertaking to establish peace on earth and good will to men throughout the world, when at this very moment nations are in civil combat and are armed to the teeth; and yet, we may take comfort from the old adage that "dripping water wears away the hardest stone." All great movements had their small beginnings, and as the acorn which falls into a crevice in the rock gradually and eventually splits the great stone wide open, so if we are persistent in our effort, certainly our dream of world peace will someday be realized. (Rotary Club, 43rd District, July 1936)

WEALTH

I am not against wealth, and I like to see people enjoy the blessings of this earth. Wealth ethically acquired and properly used is not evil—it is good. It is the love of it, the coveting of it, the lust for it, the compromises made for it which are evil. (Beneficial Life convention, San Diego, California, 1966)

Man can be miserable under the best government and happy under the worst; he can be joyous without luxuries and almost without necessities and may be discontented and in misery surrounded with wealth and its attendant comforts, if he is without hope and without a satisfied soul. (Ft. Thomas High School baccalaureate, Ft. Thomas, Arizona, 14 May 1963)

Wealth does not guarantee happiness. The abundant life, of course, has little to do with the acquisition of material things, though there are many wonderful individuals who have been blessed materially and who use their wealth to help their fellowmen—and this is most commendable. The abundant life noted in the scriptures is the spiritual sum that is arrived at by the multiplying of our service to others and by investing our talents in service to God and to man. ("The Abundant Life," *Ensign,* July 1978, 3)

What honor is there in being the richest man in the cemetery? (Letter, undated)

Why should it be so hard for rich men to enter the kingdom? Wealth should give a man independence, time, and opportunity to serve others and worship his God. It should give him a chance to alleviate suffering, teach righteousness, and further all good works.

But frequently it seems to accentuate selfishness, encourage aloofness, create class distinction, and it too often blinds its possessor to the opportunity of uncompensated service to those who cannot reward him. ("When Is One Rich?" *Salt Lake Tribune-Telegram,* 28 May 1949)

WELFARE

Welfare Services is the full program the Lord has provided us—provident living, personal and family preparedness, home and visiting teaching, producing and distributing goods to the poor, rehabilitating members with especially difficult needs or handicaps, securing jobs for the unemployed, restoring emotionally disturbed souls to full activity in the Church and society, with all of us consecrating our lives to the building up of the kingdom of God on earth. ("The Fruit of Our Welfare Services Labor," *Ensign,* Nov. 1978, 74)

WOMEN

To be a righteous woman during the winding-up scenes on this earth, before the Second Coming of our Savior, is an especially noble calling. The righteous woman's strength and influence today can be ten fold what it might be in more tranquil times. She has been placed here to help to enrich, to protect, and to guard the home—which is society's basic and most noble institution. Other institutions in society may falter and even fail, but the righteous woman can help to save the home, which may be the last and only sanctuary some mortals know in the midst of storm and strife. ("The True Way of Life and Salvation," *Ensign,* May 1978, 4)

God bless the women, the wonderful women of every time and age and place, who establish first in their lives their Lord, His work, and their families. ("Women, Wonderful Women!" *Relief Society Magazine,* Jan. 1958, 4)

It is true of all of us that, as we progress spiritually, our sense of belonging, identity, and self-worth increases. Let us create a climate in which we encourage the sisters of the Church to have a program of personal improvement. It ought to be a practical and realistic program, which is determined personally and not imposed upon them. Yet it ought to cause them to reach for new levels of achievement. We are not asking for something spectacular but rather for the women of the Church to find real self-fulfillment through wise self-development in the pursuit of righteous and worthy endeavors. ("Privileges and Responsibilities of Sisters," *Ensign,* Nov. 1978, 102)

What is our greatest potential? Is it not to achieve godhood ourselves? And what are the qualities we must develop to achieve such greatness? We might consider some: First, intelligence, light and knowledge. What special opportunities do women have in this area? These qualities, you will remember, are part of the promise given to the sisters by the Prophet Joseph Smith. Since we learn best by teaching others, we think our Relief Society sisters see the fulfillment of that promise daily as they teach children at home, in Sunday School, in Primary, in Relief Societies, in sacrament meetings, and in daily conversation. We urge our sisters who are called to teach to magnify their callings through study and prayer, recognizing the eternal values they are building for themselves, as well as for those they teach. We encourage all our sisters to take advantage of their opportunities to receive light and knowledge in school, in personal study, and in Relief Society. ("Relief Society: Its Promise and Potential," *Ensign,* March 1976, 2)

We want our homes to be blessed with sister scriptorians—whether you are single or married, young or old, widowed or living in a family. ("The Role of Righteous Women," *Ensign,* Nov. 1979, 102)

We want our women to be well educated, for children may not recover from the ignorance of their mothers. ("The Most Perfect Personage Was the Most Perfect Teacher," Seminary and Institute Teachers Conference, 12 Sept. 1975)

WORD OF WISDOM

Arguments [for allowing traffic in liquor] are specious, but to the gullible, unsuspecting, righteous, busy people, they are made to seem plausible. The tax argument, the employment one, the school lunch program, the freedom to do as one pleases— all are like sieves with many holes. There is just enough truth in them to deceive. Satan deals in half truths. ("Liquor: The Devil in Solution," *Improvement Era,* Dec. 1967, 52)

People need help who feel that a party cannot be held, a celebration enjoyed, without liquor. What a sad admission that a party must have liquor for people to have a good time. How barren must some guests be if they must be inebriated! ("Liquor: The Devil in Solution," *Improvement Era,* Dec. 1967, 52)

The Lord has insisted upon our refraining from the use of liquor, tobacco, and tea and coffee. I am sure that such abstinence will increase the length of our lives and increase the vigor of our lives. But I am sure that a deeper value comes from the observance of the Word of Wisdom than the mere length of life, for after all we must finally all pass away. The time will come when our bodies and spirits are separated, and our bodies will be laid in Mother Earth to go through the regular process, and though we do wish to continue our mortal existence as long as we can consistently, I am confident that there are greater blessings which will come to us than the strictly physical.

When I refrain from the use of these forbidden things, I am obeying my Heavenly Father, and whether or not I understand the purpose, I will still receive the blessing. ("The Spirit Giveth Life," *Improvement Era,* Dec. 1951, 899)

WORK

"What can we do?" children ask.

Do the shopping, work in the hospital, help the neighbors and the church custodian, wash dishes, vacuum the floors, make the beds, get the meals, learn to sew.

Read good books, repair the furniture, make something needed in the home, clean the house, press your clothes, rake the leaves, shovel the snow, peddle papers, do "baby-sitting" free for neighbor mothers who must work, become an apprentice. ("Keep Mothers in the Home," *Improvement Era,* Dec. 1963, 1071)

Those tremendously useful men, those powerful and invincible men—Marconi, Edison, the Wright Brothers, Burbank—who sit wrapped in purple robes of creative genius, are simply men who are capable of striking reiterated blows. They are men who reached success because they subjected themselves to the fierce fires of intellectual and physical endeavor. Men never ascend to eminence by a single leap or by growth overnight. Longfellow wrote, "The heights by great men reached and kept were not attained by sudden flight, but they, while their companions slept, were toiling upward in the night." (Virden High School commencement, Virden, New Mexico, 20 May 1932)

We want you parents to create work for your children. Insist on them learning their lessons in school. Do not let them play all the time. There is a time for play, there is a time to work, and there is a time to study. Be sure your children grow up like you know they ought to grow. You know what happens to people who coast along—they just get in a boat and have no oars nor sails nor engine. They float down the river and the current just carries them down gradually until they come down into the swamps. (Conference of Indians in southern Utah stakes, St. George, UT, April 1960)

WORSHIP

Man is naturally a religious being. His heart instinctively seeks for God whether he reverences the sacred cow or prays to the sun or moon; whether he kneels before wood and stone images, or prays in secret to his Heavenly Father, he is satisfying an inborn urge. (Eastern Arizona College baccalaureate, Thatcher, Arizona, May 1963)

ZION

Zion can be built up only among those who are the pure in heart, not a people torn by covetousness or greed, but a pure and selfless people. Not a people who are pure in appearance, rather a people who are pure in heart. Zion is to be in the world and not of the world, not dulled by a sense of carnal security, nor paralyzed by materialism. No, Zion is not things of the lower, but of the higher order, things that exalt the mind and sanctify the heart.

Zion is "every man seeking the interest of his neighbor, and doing all things with an eye single to the glory of God." (D&C 82:19.) ("Becoming the Pure in Heart," *Ensign,* May 1978, 79)